THE *NEW* SCIENCE OF GETTING RICH

ALSO BY ROBERT T. YARBOROUGH

Beyond Space and Time

Getting Down to Brass Tacks

The Outrage Paradox

The Self Coaching Blueprint

Quantum Whispers

Be Done With It

COMING SOON
The New Science of Being Great

THE *NEW* SCIENCE OF GETTING RICH

A Modern Guide to to Effortless Wealth and Abundance

Based on theTimeless Principles of Wallace D. Wattles

Robert T. Yarborough

Pranava Books

Disclaimer: This book is intended for informational and educational purposes only. The ideas, practices, and suggestions presented in this book are based on personal experiences, research, and insights. They are not a substitute for professional medical, psychological, or financial advice.

While every effort has been made to ensure the accuracy and completeness of the information, the author and publisher make no representations or warranties of any kind, express or implied, about the completeness, accuracy, reliability, suitability, or availability with respect to the information, products, services, or related graphics contained in this book for any purpose.

Readers are encouraged to consult qualified professionals for advice tailored to their individual circumstances. The author and publisher disclaim any liability arising directly or indirectly from the application or misapplication of the information contained in this book.

Your journey is unique—use the tools and concepts shared here as a guide to create your own path.

Publisher's Cataloging-in-Publication Data

Yarborough, Robert T., 1960–
The New Science of Getting Rich: A Modern Guide to Wallace D. Wattles' Timeless Principles for Wealth and Abundance/ Robert T. Yarborough, based on the original work by Wallace D. Wattles (1860–1911).
— First edition.
p. cm.
ISBN: 979-8-9912582-2-7

    1.. Wealth—Psychological aspects. 2. Success—Psychology. 3. Self-actualization (Psychology). 4. Personal development. 5. Prosperity consciousness. I. Wattles, Wallace D., 1860–1911. The Science of Getting Rich. II. Title.
BF637.S8 Y37 2025
   158.1 — dc23
LCCN: 2025901981

Printed in the United States of America
10 9 8 7 6 5 4 3 2 1

Table of Contents

The Original Unedited Version   85

This book is based on The Science of Getting Rich by Wallace D. Wattles, originally published in 1910. This modern adaptation has been expanded, revised, and updated with contemporary language, insights, and applications. While the core principles of Wattles' work remain foundational, this version represents a unique and original reinterpretation.

Author's Preface

We live in a world of infinite potential, yet so many people feel trapped—trapped by circumstances, by scarcity, by fear. For over a century, *The Science of Getting Rich* has been a beacon of hope, guiding individuals toward financial success through disciplined thinking and acting. Wallace D. Wattles' timeless work introduced the idea that wealth is not random, nor is it a privilege granted to a select few; rather, it is a process governed by universal principles that, when understood and applied, produce results as certainly as gravity pulls objects to the ground.

This new edition honors the original wisdom of Wattles while modernizing its language and deepening its insights. In an age where distractions are constant and misinformation about wealth abounds, refining our understanding of abundance is more important than ever. Many people speak of "manifestation" as if it were magic, but Wattles did not teach wishful thinking. He taught a *method*, a systematic approach to wealth grounded in thought, gratitude, faith, and action. This edition expands upon those teachings with contemporary clarity, integrating mindfulness, neuroscience, and the deeper spiritual truths that align with his original message.

The purpose of this book is simple: to help you understand and apply *the science* of getting rich. Not luck. Not force. Not mere positive thinking. But a definite, structured approach to financial and personal expansion. This book is not about competitive wealth—where one person's gain is another's loss—but creative wealth, where all expansion contributes to life itself. When you understand and apply this science, you not only transform your own life but you uplift those around you.

Why Modernize This Book?

Wattles' work was revolutionary, and its truths remain as powerful today. However, modern readers need more than a new typesetting of old words—they need deeper clarity, real-world application, and a bridge between timeless wisdom and today's challenges. This new version does not change the principles—it refines them, ensuring that the power of his words is not just read but *lived*.

What You Will Discover

Within these pages, you will find:

- A clear explanation of the universal laws that govern wealth and success.

- The mental discipline required to align yourself with abundance.

- The role of gratitude in creating lasting prosperity.

- How to take action in a way that guarantees success.

- Why competition leads to lack, while creation leads to limitless wealth.

- How faith and purpose shape reality as surely as physical effort.

◆ Practical exercises to integrate these principles into your daily life.

This book is not a passive read. It is a guide to *becoming*— becoming the person who naturally attracts wealth, contributes meaningfully to the world, and steps beyond limitations into an ever-expanding life.

A Final Thought Before We Begin

If you have ever struggled with money, doubted your ability to succeed, or felt that life was happening *to* you instead of *through* you—this book is for you. It is an invitation to see wealth not as something outside of you but as something you are aligned with through your thoughts, intentions, and actions.

The principles in this book are not theory—they are a practice. And when practiced with faith and persistence, they will lead you to the realization that wealth is not a privilege nor a matter of chance. It is a law. It is science. And it is yours to claim.

Now, let us begin.

INTRODUCTION

"Your thoughts are the architects of your destiny."

— David O. McKay

It happens in a moment.

You wake up one morning, stretch, and realize—*really* realize—that nothing has changed.

The same problems. The same worries. The same nagging thoughts pull at the edges of your mind before your feet even touch the floor. You were hoping today would feel different. Lighter, maybe. But the weight is still there, pressing against your chest, invisible but suffocating.

You roll out of bed, already anticipating the battle ahead. Maybe it's the job you hate but can't afford to leave. Maybe the debt seems to grow faster than you can shrink it. Maybe it's the gnawing feeling that no matter how hard you try, you're always behind, always scrambling, always reaching for something just beyond your grasp.

The world tells you to work harder. To hustle. To sacrifice more sleep, more time, more of yourself. But what if that's the problem?

What if everything you've been told about success, about money, about *getting ahead*—is wrong?

The Silent Struggle No One Talks About

It's easy to feel like you're the only one stuck in this endless cycle. On the outside, it looks like everyone else has it figured out. Friends post pictures of dream vacations, new cars, and promotions. Strangers on social media flaunt lifestyles that seem impossibly out of reach. You scroll through, telling yourself you're happy for them, but deep down, something twists inside you.

"Why not me?"

"What am I doing wrong?"

"Will it always be like this?"

And maybe the hardest thought of all—the one you barely admit to yourself—*Maybe I'm just not meant for more.*

The world has a way of making struggle feel personal. If you're not where you want to be, it must be because you didn't try hard enough. You weren't smart enough. You weren't born into the right circumstances. You weren't lucky.

And so you push harder. Work longer. Try to be more disciplined, more strategic, more *something*—but no matter what you do, it never seems to be enough.

Somewhere along the way, you start to wonder if this is just how life is. If struggle, stress, and exhaustion are inevitable. If peace, joy, and security are things reserved for *other* people.

But what if they aren't?

What if everything you believe about why you feel stuck isn't true?

The Turning Point No One Sees Coming

There's a moment in every person's life when something shifts. It rarely comes with fanfare. No flashing lights. No neon signs pointing the way. More often, it sneaks up on you in the quiet moments—when you're lying awake at 2 AM, staring at the ceiling, or sitting in traffic, gripping the steering wheel a little too tightly.

It's the moment you realize you *can't keep living like this.*

Maybe you don't know the way forward yet. Maybe you don't have the answers. But deep down, something inside you whispers:

"There has to be more than this."

That whisper is important.

That whisper is everything.

Because it's the first crack in the wall.

For the first time, you question what you've always assumed to be true. The beliefs that have shaped your life. The invisible rules you've followed without ever asking, *Who wrote these rules?*

And in that questioning, something remarkable happens.

You begin to see that what's been keeping you stuck isn't a lack of effort, intelligence, or worthiness.

It's a story.

A story you've been told. A story you've been repeating to yourself without even realizing it.

A story that has never been true.

The Door You Never Noticed Before

Imagine walking down the same hallway every day of your life. The walls are lined with doors, but you don't notice them. You've been told there's only one way forward, so you keep walking straight ahead, following the path everyone else is on.

But then, one day, something changes.

You stop.

You turn your head—just slightly—and for the first time, you see a door you never noticed before. It was there the whole time, but you were so focused on moving forward, on *trying harder*, that you never saw it.

And now, the question is:

Do you keep walking the same path?

Or do you stop, turn the handle, and step into something new?

That's where you are right now.

Standing at a door you didn't know existed.

And what's on the other side is something you can't yet imagine—but you can feel it.

A lightness. A freedom. A way of moving through life where struggle is no longer the default setting.

Not because you've worked yourself to exhaustion. Not because you've out-hustled or outsmarted anyone.

But because you've stepped out of the old way of thinking.

You've *unlearned* what was never true.

And in its place, you've discovered something that changes everything.

That door is open.

All you have to do is step through.

That moment of realization—the one where you see the door—can feel exhilarating. But it can also be terrifying.

Because if it was always there, if a different way of living, thinking, and *being* was always an option, then what does that say about everything you've believed up until now?

What does that say about the years spent following the rules, doing what you were *supposed* to do, and still ending up feeling stuck, overwhelmed, or behind?

It's not your fault.

You weren't given the right map.

You were handed a blueprint designed for limitation. It is a story written by people who were trapped in the same patterns, the same fear, and the same narrow version of what's possible.

But now, you have a choice.

And in these pages, you're going to be given something radically different.

What You Are About to Learn Will Change the Way You See Everything

This is not a book about working harder. It's not about pushing yourself past exhaustion, sacrificing joy, or following yet another formula that promises results but leaves you feeling emptier than before.

This is not about getting rich in the way the world has conditioned you to think about wealth.

Because *rich* isn't just money in the bank.

It's a feeling. A way of existing in the world. A deep, unshakable knowing that life is working with you, not against you. That abundance isn't something to chase—it's something you allow.

You will not be told to grind yourself into the ground.

You will not be told that success belongs only to the lucky, the privileged, or the ruthless.

Instead, you will learn a way of thinking and being that aligns you with something much more powerful. A way of shifting your perspective so that the opportunities, ideas, and resources that once seemed out of reach begin to flow toward you—effortlessly.

You will learn why the struggle you've experienced wasn't because you weren't smart enough, disciplined enough, or deserving enough.

You will learn how the energy you hold—your thoughts, your emotions, your expectations—acts as a signal, shaping your experiences in ways you may never have realized before.

And most importantly, you will learn how to break free.

Not in some vague, mystical way. But through a process that is as practical as it is profound. A process that has been quietly transforming lives for over a century is now refined and expanded with the wisdom of modern insight.

This is not about wishing.

This is about *knowing*.

It's about stepping into a state where your very presence shifts the world around you.

Where wealth—financial, emotional, and spiritual—becomes not something to chase but something that naturally flows toward you.

And if you think that sounds too good to be true, ask yourself this:

What if the only reason it hasn't been true for you yet is because you've never allowed yourself to believe it could be?

Why I Can Tell You This with Absolute Certainty

I was once where you are now.

I know what it's like to feel stuck in a life that doesn't quite fit, to look around and wonder if maybe some people were just meant for more while others were meant to struggle.

I spent years trying to do things the *right* way—working harder, pushing through exhaustion, following every piece of conventional wisdom about success and wealth.

And yet, something was always missing.

The results were inconsistent. The stress was constant. The joy? Fleeting at best.

And then, something changed.

Not through luck. Not through some secret, elite strategy.

But through a shift in perception so simple, so fundamental, that it seemed almost *too* easy.

I didn't learn it from a business seminar or a motivational guru. I found it in the unlikeliest of places—inside myself.

It was there all along.

And once I saw it, once I *felt* it, everything changed.

The struggle stopped.

Opportunities began appearing—not because I forced them, but because I was finally open to receiving them.

Money, success, abundance—it all came, but not in the way I had been taught to expect, not through exhaustion and effort, but through alignment.

And I realized: *this is what no one is telling us.*

This is why so many people work themselves into the ground, only to find themselves feeling just as empty, just as anxious, just as unfulfilled as before.

Because they are chasing something that cannot be chased.

It can only be *allowed.*

The Shift That Changes Everything

You've felt glimpses of it before.

The days when things just *clicked* into place. When an opportunity arises at just the right moment. When an unexpected windfall arrives just as you need it.

You may have called it a coincidence. Luck. Divine intervention.

But what if it wasn't any of those things?

What if it was *you*—not by accident, but by the rare moment when you stopped resisting and let life flow?

What if that wasn't supposed to be rare at all?

The difference between those who struggle and those who seem to live effortlessly isn't intelligence. It isn't background or talent.

It's something much simpler, much more fundamental.

It's the ability to *see*—to recognize the hidden patterns that shape reality and to shift into a way of thinking, being, and acting that aligns with those patterns rather than fights against them.

This book is going to show you how.

Not with vague ideas or empty promises, but with a perspective so clear, so immediately transformative, that once you see it, you will *never* be able to unsee it.

You are not here to scrape by.

You are not here to trade your life away for the illusion of security.

You are here to thrive.

And everything you need to do that is already within you.

Now, all that's left is for you to remember.

To wake up to the truth that has been waiting for you all along.

And once you do, you'll never go back.

ONE

The Right to Be Rich

"When I was young, I thought that money was the most important thing in life; now that I am old, I know that it is."

— Oscar Wilde

The notion that poverty is virtuous is an illusion, a deeply ingrained belief that has led many to accept lack as their fate. But if you observe life itself, you will see that all living things strive for expansion, for more, for the fullest expression of their being. The tree reaches for the sky, the river seeks the ocean, the flower turns toward the sun. Life, in its essence, moves toward greater expression, not contraction. So too, the human being is meant to grow, to expand, to thrive—and wealth is an essential part of this process.

To be truly alive is to engage fully with existence. This engagement requires resources—money, yes, but more importantly, the ability to access what is needed to nourish the mind, the body, and the soul. Without wealth, one's capacity for development is stunted. Imagine trying to cultivate wisdom while struggling to meet basic survival needs. Imagine attempting to create art, to write, to teach, or to innovate while consumed by financial worry. True fulfillment requires a state of ease, a foundation from which one can explore, expand, and evolve.

The pursuit of wealth is not about greed, nor is it about acquiring material possessions for their own sake. It is about aligning with the natural flow of abundance, recognizing that money is simply a tool for living more fully. To deny yourself wealth is to deny yourself the resources that enable growth, learning, and the ability to contribute meaningfully to the world.

Wealth as the Natural State

There is a common belief that one must choose between wealth and spirituality, between material success and inner peace. But this is a false dichotomy. Wealth and spiritual fulfillment are not opposing forces—they are complementary. The soul expresses itself most freely when the burdens of lack are lifted. The body thrives when it is well-nourished, rested, and free from unnecessary stress. The mind flourishes when it has the time, space, and means to explore its full potential. To live fully is to live abundantly in all aspects—materially, intellectually, and spiritually.

To seek wealth is not selfish. It is natural. The desire to have more, to experience more, and to be more is the same impulse that drives the universe to expand. When you are rich, you are not taking from others—you are allowing yourself to participate more fully in the great unfolding of life. The more you have, the more you can give. The more you experience, the more you can share. The more you grow, the more you inspire others to do the same. True wealth is not accumulation; it is circulation, a continuous flow of energy and opportunity.

The Right to Abundance

You have the right to be rich because you have the right to live fully. Every human being is born with infinite potential, yet that potential can only manifest when it is given the space and resources to do so. Consider a seed: it contains within it the blueprint for a towering tree, but without sunlight, water, and nutrients from the soil, it will remain dormant. In the same way, you contain within you the potential for greatness, but that potential requires nourishment in the form of education, experiences, and material well-being.

This is not about indulgence. It is about alignment. When you align yourself with the natural laws of abundance, wealth flows into your life with ease. It does not require struggle, nor does it require deprivation. It requires awareness—an understanding that the universe is abundant, that opportunities are limitless, and that scarcity is an illusion created by those who have forgotten their own power.

Wealth as a Means of Expression

To be truly wealthy is not just to have money; it is to be free to express your highest self. To love without limitation. To create without restriction. To give without hesitation. A rich life is one in which you can pursue your passions, support those you care about, and contribute to the world in a way that is meaningful to you. It is not merely about having but about being—being at peace, being expansive, being fully engaged in the experience of life.

Recognizing your right to be rich is the first step. The next is understanding that wealth is not something outside of you, something to be chased or earned through sheer effort. It is something you step into, something you allow. It begins with the realization that abundance is already here, already present in the very fabric of existence. Your task is not to struggle for it but to open yourself to it.

The Responsibility of Wealth

With the right to wealth comes responsibility. Not in the sense of burden but in the sense of purpose. The more you have, the more you can uplift others. The more you grow, the more you can help others grow. The more you create, the more you add to the richness of the world. This is not about guilt or obligation; it is about joy. There is joy in giving, joy in sharing, joy in contributing to the expansion of life itself.

You have the right to be rich, not as a privilege, but as a birthright. You were not born to live in lack or limitation. You were born to thrive. To learn the science of getting rich is to learn the science of living fully, of embracing all that life has to offer. It is not a pursuit of money for its own sake but a pursuit of wholeness, of balance, of complete self-expression.

When you embrace this truth, you will find that wealth is not something you acquire; it is something you become. And as you become rich—rich in mind, rich in body, rich in soul—you will naturally bring more richness into the world.

TWO

THE SCIENCE OF GETTING RICH

"Success is not a matter of luck. It is a matter of knowing what you want, doing what you need to do, and believing you will get there."

— Tony Robbins

Wealth is not an accident. It is not something that happens to some while eluding others without reason. There is an underlying intelligence, a structure, a pattern to the creation of abundance. Just as the universe operates under laws of gravity, motion, and energy, so too does the accumulation of wealth follow specific principles. When you align yourself with these principles, you step into the natural flow of abundance.

Many believe that riches are the result of luck, talent, or external circumstances, yet observe carefully, and you will see that wealth appears in all walks of life. Some are born into poverty and rise to prosperity, while others inherit fortune and squander it. The determining factor is not intelligence, skill, or birthright—it is whether one operates in harmony with the laws that govern abundance. These laws are as precise as those of mathematics; once understood and applied, wealth follows with certainty.

The Certain Way

To achieve wealth, one must do things in a Certain Way. This way is not about working harder than others, nor is it about taking advantage of external opportunities. It is about aligning with the deeper order of life, recognizing that wealth flows naturally to those who act in harmony with its principles.

It is not effort alone that brings riches, for many work tirelessly and remain in struggle. Nor is it talent, for many gifted individuals find themselves in lack while those of average ability prosper. Wealth does not arise from saving every penny, for the most frugal often remain poor, while free spenders sometimes amass fortunes. The key lies in a deeper understanding—that doing things in a Certain Way is what makes the difference.

The Illusion of External Limitations

If wealth were dependent solely on environment, then everyone in a prosperous area would be rich and everyone in a struggling area would be poor. Yet we see that in the same location, under the same conditions, one man flourishes while another falters. This is clear evidence that abundance is not a matter of place but of alignment.

Similarly, talent alone is not the determinant of riches. If it were, the most intelligent, the most artistic, and the most skilled would dominate the ranks of wealth. Yet we see many with extraordinary gifts who live in poverty while others, seemingly ordinary, rise to great prosperity. The conclusion is unavoidable: wealth is not about location, talent, or luck—it is about whether one acts in harmony with the unseen principles of abundance.

Cause and Effect in Wealth Creation

There is no randomness in the universe. Like causes always produce like effects. Just as planting a seed in fertile soil, giving it water and sunlight inevitably results in growth, so too does aligning oneself with the laws of abundance inevitably results in wealth. The difficulty for many is not in whether this principle is true but in whether they are applying it.

To bring forth riches, one must cultivate a mind aligned with abundance rather than scarcity. Fear, doubt, and resentment create resistance, cutting one off from the natural flow of prosperity. Those who focus on lack will experience more lack, while those who see and act in accordance with opportunity will attract more opportunities.

The Universality of Wealth

Some may wonder whether this Certain Way is difficult, accessible only to a select few. But the laws of wealth, like all universal principles, are impartial and available to all. Strong and weak, intelligent and foolish, educated and uneducated— all can attain prosperity if they do things in the Certain Way.

It is not a question of one's starting point. If wealth requires prior wealth, then no one can rise from poverty. Yet history is filled with examples of those who began with nothing and ascended to financial freedom. The conditions of one's life at this moment are not barriers; they are merely the starting point.

The Path to Wealth

If one is in the wrong profession, they can transition to the right one. If they lack capital, they can attract it. If they are in the wrong location, they can move or create opportunities where they are. But none of this happens by force, struggle, or wishful thinking. It happens by beginning where one is, doing things in the Certain Way that aligns with abundance.

Wealth is a matter of cause and effect. When you shift your thoughts, your actions, and your state of being into harmony with the principles of abundance, prosperity must follow. It is not a question of whether the laws will work for you—they are always working. The only question is whether you are working with them or against them.

In the chapters ahead, we will explore how to align fully with this Certain Way. For now, recognize that your current conditions do not define your potential. The path to abundance is always open. The laws of wealth, like all universal laws, do not fail.

THREE

Is Opportunity Monopolized?

"Do not wait to strike till the iron is hot;
but make it hot by striking."

— William Butler Yeats

The idea that wealth is controlled by a select few and opportunity is fenced off by the powerful is an illusion. The mind that believes itself to be shut out from abundance will experience limitation, but the truth is that no one is inherently excluded. Opportunity is not static; it flows, changes, and manifests in infinite ways. While one avenue may seem closed, countless others remain open, waiting to be recognized.

You may look at certain industries, the great financial empires, and think that those who came before have locked all the doors to wealth. But this is not so. While one path may seem crowded, another is emerging. History moves forward, and new needs arise. Those who attune themselves to this movement, who recognize where the flow of opportunity is going, will always find a way.

The Ever-Present Stream of Opportunity

Consider this: at any given moment, life is expanding, seeking greater expression. Just as rivers carve new paths, wealth also shifts and flows. The question is not whether opportunity exists but whether you are awake enough to perceive it.

To insist that wealth is monopolized is to misunderstand the nature of abundance. One cannot look only at what has already been built and conclude that all space for creation is occupied. Just as new inventions replace the old, new industries rise where others have matured.

If you do not see the opportunity, it is not because it is absent but because your awareness is focused on limitation rather than expansion. When you shift your perception and become open to the unseen currents of change, you step into the infinite field of possibilities.

The Fallacy of Lack

It is easy to believe that wealth is a finite resource and that one person's gain must be another's loss. But observe nature, and you will see that life does not operate under restrictions. The tree does not hoard the air it breathes, nor does the ocean limit the number of waves that can rise upon its surface. The very fabric of existence is designed for continual renewal.

You are not kept in poverty because the world is lacking in riches. You are not denied prosperity because others have found it before you. The source from which all things come is inexhaustible. It is not diminished by use. New forms are constantly being created, and new opportunities are arising in response to the ever-evolving needs of humanity.

To see the world through the lens of scarcity is to align with scarcity. To see it through the lens of abundance is to align with infinite possibility. Your experience will reflect your perception.

The Flow of Wealth and the Power of Awareness

There is no external force keeping you from prosperity. The only force that truly holds you back is the belief that you are held back. Opportunity is not something given or withheld by others; it is something perceived and acted upon. Two people may stand in the same environment and circumstances, yet one sees limitations while the other sees infinite potential. The difference is not in the environment—it is in the mind that perceives it.

Those who understand the principles of abundance do not struggle against the tide. They do not resent the success of others or fight to take a piece of what already exists. Instead, they attune themselves to the movement of life itself, sensing where expansion is occurring and where creation is ready to emerge. They step forward to participate in its unfolding.

The Responsibility of the Individual

The idea that external conditions hold an individual back comforts the ego, but it is not true. Circumstances may present challenges, but they do not determine destiny. The determining factor is always the inner state—aligning thought, intention, and action with the reality of abundance.

If one path is closed, another is open. If one industry is saturated, another is being born. If an opportunity seems distant, it is only because you have not yet aligned yourself with it. The invitation is always present—to shift your focus, expand your awareness, and participate fully in the ever-unfolding dance of creation.

Aligning with Infinite Supply

The substance from which all things emerge is limitless. This is not a metaphor; it is a truth observable in the very nature of reality. The universe does not run out of ideas, energy, or resources. It is constantly creating, renewing, and making way for greater expression.

When you understand this, lack becomes an impossibility. You do not need to take from another, nor do you need to compete for limited resources. Your wealth does not depend on someone else's loss. Instead, you align yourself with the creative force of life itself, knowing that new avenues of opportunity are constantly forming.

The key is not to seek opportunity as if it is something outside of you, controlled by forces beyond your reach. Instead, it is to awaken to the truth that opportunity is ever-present, flowing through you, waiting for you to recognize it and step forward in faith.

The path to wealth is not closed—it has never been closed—and waits for those ready to see it.

FOUR

The First Principle in the Science of Getting Rich

"You are today where your thoughts have brought you; you will be tomorrow where your thoughts take you."

— James Allen

Everything in existence begins in thought. The physical world is not separate from the realm of ideas but is an extension of it. What you perceive as reality is the manifestation of consciousness in form, shaped by the unseen forces of intention and awareness. Just as a tree begins as a seed, so too does every aspect of wealth, abundance, and creation begin as an idea, held and impressed upon the fabric of existence.

The foundation of all riches is thought. This is not mere philosophy but a fundamental law of life. Every structure, innovation, work of art, and financial empire began as an idea. In its infinite intelligence, the universe moves in alignment with thought, shaping and reshaping itself according to the energy impressed upon it. The formless substance of life is responsive; it does not resist but flows into whatever form consciousness directs it toward.

The Power of Thought in Creation

You are not separate from this creative force but an extension of it. As a conscious being, you possess the ability to shape your reality through the thoughts you hold consistently. The challenge, however, is that most people do not think deliberately. They allow external appearances to dictate their mental state, reinforcing limitation instead of possibility.

To create wealth, you must first understand that your thoughts are not passive. They are the blueprint for the world you experience. If your mind is dominated by scarcity, struggle, and lack, you unknowingly shape your reality according to these patterns. But when you consciously hold thoughts of abundance, expansion, and unlimited possibility, the universe responds in kind, moving unseen forces into motion to bring forth what you have envisioned.

Thought Aligns with Universal Substance

The universe is not a static, fixed entity. It is alive, fluid, and constantly responding to consciousness. Just as a sculptor shapes clay, your thoughts shape the unseen substance from which all things emerge. To believe in lack is to misperceive reality. The true nature of existence is infinite; creation never ceases, and supply is never exhausted.

If you hold the thought of limitation, you are closing the door to possibility. If you hold the thought of expansion, you align with the flow of life itself. The secret is to think not according to appearances but according to truth. The appearance of scarcity is an illusion created by unconscious belief. The reality is that abundance is ever-present, waiting to be realized.

The Mastery of Thought

Most people allow their minds to be shaped by external conditions. They believe in wealth when they see it but doubt it when appearances suggest otherwise. This is reactive thinking. True mastery begins when you understand that thought precedes form, not the other way around.

To think what you choose to think, regardless of external conditions, is the beginning of self-mastery. This is not an easy task; it requires inner discipline and awareness. It is far easier to be carried by the tides of collective thinking, to see poverty and accept it as truth, to experience difficulty and assume it is the final reality. But the mind that remains fixed on truth rather than illusion begins to shape the world according to that truth.

The Three Fundamental Truths

There are three principles that must be accepted fully if you are to understand and apply the science of getting rich:

1. **There is an intelligent, formless substance from which all things emerge.** This substance is infinite, ever-present, and constantly responding to thought. It permeates all of existence and is the foundation of everything you see and experience.

2. **A thought held in this substance produces the form of that thought.** The universe does not question or resist; it simply responds. Whatever is consistently impressed upon the formless substance will take shape in due time.

3. You have the ability to consciously direct your thoughts to shape reality. This is the greatest power given to humanity—the ability to create through thought. You are not at the mercy of circumstances; you are a creator within the vast intelligence of the universe.

The Discipline of Thought

Many will struggle with these truths, not because they are difficult to understand, but because they contradict the conditioned beliefs that have been absorbed over a lifetime. To look upon limitation and still hold the thought of abundance requires strength. To experience financial hardship and still think prosperity is an act of profound mastery.

You must train your mind to hold truth unwaveringly. The moment you allow doubt, fear, or external appearances to dictate your thinking, you sever your alignment with the creative force. But when you remain steadfast and refuse to accept lack as reality, the unseen energies of the universe move in your favor. What was once invisible begins to take form.

A New Way of Seeing

To live in the awareness of these truths is to move beyond conventional perception. It is to see not only with your eyes but with your inner knowing. What appears as empty space is filled with infinite creative substance. What appears as limitation is simply the illusion of an untrained mind. The world is not fixed—it is fluid, dynamic, and constantly reshaping itself according to the thoughts impressed upon it.

This is the first principle in the science of getting rich: thought is the foundation of all creation. Wealth, health, success—everything you seek—begins with the thoughts you hold in mind. Align with the truth of infinite abundance, and you will begin to shape your life in ways you once thought impossible.

We'd Love to Hear From You!

Thank you so much for reading this book-it means the world to me. If you found it helpful, inspiring, or just enjoyable, would you take a moment to leave a review? Your feedback not only helps others but also keeps me motivated to create more valuable content for you.

Here's how you can leave a review:

1. Scan the QR code on this page to go directly to the author's page.

2. Or, visit your Amazon Orders page, find this book, and click "Write a Product Review."

**Your kind words make a big difference.
Thank you for your support!**

FIVE

INCREASING LIFE

"Progress is impossible without change, and those who cannot change their minds cannot change anything."

— George Bernard Shaw

You must release the last remnants of the old belief that poverty serves a divine purpose or that scarcity is the natural order of existence. The intelligence that pervades all things—the conscious, living presence within you and around you—exists for expansion, for the increase of life itself. The very nature of life is to grow, become more, and express more. This is the essence of abundance.

Consider nature: when planted, a single seed does not remain one seed. It multiplies, producing a hundred more. Life begets life. It is in the act of living that life expands. So, too, intelligence is bound to this principle. Every thought leads to another thought, every discovery paves the way for new understanding, and every talent cultivated awakens the desire for further mastery. Life, by its nature, seeks expression. To suppress this expansion is to go against the very force that sustains existence.

The Desire for More is Natural

The desire for greater wealth is not greed—it is life seeking a fuller expression through you. It is the same force that makes a tree reach for the sun, that drives a river to carve new paths, that propels the cosmos to expand infinitely. The intelligence that governs all things is infused with the necessity of growth, and because you are an extension of that intelligence, you too are compelled to seek increase.

This is why you must never regard the desire to be rich as something impure. It is not about accumulating possessions for their own sake or indulging in fleeting pleasures. It is about having the means to fully participate in life—to explore, create, contribute, and experience joy. To deny yourself wealth is to deny life's natural movement toward expansion.

The Universe Supports Your Expansion

The universe desires for you what you desire for yourself. The intelligence that created galaxies, forests, and oceans is not indifferent to your aspirations. It seeks to express more through you, to live more through you. The world's resources are not meant to be hoarded by a select few, nor are they reserved only for those who came before you. They are infinite, replenished by the same intelligence that brought them into being.

You do not need to compete. You do not need to take from others. The wealth you seek does not come by diminishing what already exists but by calling forth new creation. You are here to be a creator, not a competitor. The more you expand, the more the whole of existence expands with you.

Aligning with Life's Purpose

True wealth is not about excess or mindless indulgence. It is about balance. The fullest life is one in which all aspects—physical, mental, and spiritual—are harmoniously engaged. Denying the body's needs in pursuit of the mind is imbalance. Seeking only material wealth without wisdom leads to emptiness. Focusing solely on spiritual growth while neglecting the means to live fully in the world is incomplete.

To live fully means to express all aspects of yourself without limitation. You seek wealth not to escape life but to engage in it completely. You desire money not to dominate or compare but to create, experience, and uplift. This is why aligning your purpose with the greater purpose that moves through all things is essential.

Wealth is Not Taken—It is Created

Many people fall into the illusion that a select few control riches, that opportunities are scarce, and that one must compete for limited resources. This is not so. Wealth is not something that must be taken—it is something that is formed. The same intelligence that created the gold in the earth and the trees in the forest is the same intelligence that continues to generate new opportunities, new ideas, and new avenues for prosperity.

When you align yourself with this truth, you release the scarcity mindset. You stop believing that others hold your destiny in their hands. You no longer see wealth as something that must be wrestled away from others. Instead, you recognize that by thinking in harmony with the laws of abundance, you cause new wealth to be created—not only for yourself but for the greater whole.

Let Go of Competition and Embrace Creation

The moment you believe that success is about outpacing others, you align with limitation. You begin to see yourself as separate, disconnected from the infinite creative force that sustains all things. You become trapped in the illusion of lack. But when you recognize that the universe is abundant beyond measure, you step into a space where opportunities are limitless, and new wealth is always waiting to be born through your thoughts and actions.

It is unnecessary to outmaneuver, manipulate, or struggle against others. The wealth that is yours is already forming within the unseen substance of life, waiting to take shape through your alignment with it. No one else's success diminishes your own. No one else's prosperity takes away from what is available to you. Let go of competition. Focus instead on creation.

The Power of Knowing

You must cultivate absolute certainty that your wealth is already forming. Do not fixate on visible supply; what you see is merely a fraction of what exists. The universe is vast, and its resources are without end. There is no limit to the ideas, the opportunities, the material wealth that can come into being. Your task is not to doubt but to know.

Know that the means for your expansion are already set in motion. Know that the universe is working in perfect harmony to bring you all you need. Know that you do not need to struggle but rather align your thoughts, actions, and state of being with the infinite abundance already here.

A Life of Continuous Growth

You are not here to stay the same. You are here to expand, express more life, and become more than you have ever been. Wealth is not something external to chase; it is the natural byproduct of living in alignment with the increasing force of life itself. When you commit to this path, you step into a flow where all things are added unto you—not by force but by the effortless unfolding of a life lived in harmony with abundance.

Never doubt. Never fear. Know that all you seek is already seeking you. The journey is not about acquiring—it is about becoming. And as you become more, you will naturally bring more life to yourself and the world around you. This is the true meaning of wealth. This is the increasing life.

SIX

How Riches Come to You

"You can have everything in life you want, if you will just help other people get what they want."

— Zig Ziglar

Riches do not come through force or manipulation. They do not require struggle, competition, or the exploitation of others. Wealth flows naturally when you align yourself with the creative power of life and when you understand that abundance is not something to be taken—it is something to be received.

You are not separate from the world around you. The same intelligence that moves the tides that cause trees to grow and stars to shine also moves through you. This intelligence is always expanding, always seeking greater expression. It wants to live more fully through you; to do that, it provides all that you need. The only question is whether you are open to receiving it.

The Exchange of Value

To receive wealth, you must understand the principle of giving more in use value than you take in cash value. This does not mean undervaluing yourself or sacrificing your own well-being for the benefit of others. It means that every transaction you engage in should add life to you and those you interact with.

If someone purchases a book for a few dollars and that book changes their life, have they not received more in return than what they spent? True wealth creation is not about extracting from others but expanding life through the exchange of value.

If you are engaged in business, ask yourself: Are you providing something that enriches the lives of those you serve? If so, you will never need to resort to manipulation, for the universe will naturally support that which supports life.

You Are Not in Competition

The moment you believe that wealth is limited, that success comes at the expense of another, you shift into a mindset of scarcity. In reality, wealth is created, not distributed. There is no need to struggle against others or to fear opportunities are being taken away from you.

When you act in alignment with abundance, new pathways open. The resources, ideas, and opportunities you need will be drawn to you—not through force but through the natural unfolding of life's intelligence. Those who seem to amass wealth through competition may appear successful, but their wealth is often fleeting because it is built on instability rather than creation.

The Power of Faith and Certainty

If you desire something—whether it be a new home, financial freedom, or the ability to travel—understand that the very desire itself is evidence that it is possible for you. The intelligence that placed that vision in your mind is the same intelligence that has the power to bring it into being.

But there is a key principle: You must claim what you desire with absolute certainty. Once you form the thought, hold onto it with unwavering faith. Do not doubt. Do not entertain thoughts of impossibility. Know that what you have envisioned is already moving toward you, and act according to that knowledge.

This does not mean waiting passively. It means moving through life with confidence, taking inspired action, and trusting that the universe is orchestrating events in ways you cannot yet see.

Creation, Not Chance

Riches do not appear randomly. They are the result of thought directed with intention. If you truly grasp this, you will see that wealth is not reserved for a select few. It is available to anyone who aligns their mind with abundance.

You are not required to understand the exact path by which your desires will come to you. The means are not your concern. Your only responsibility is to hold the vision, believe in the certainty of its arrival, and take actions aligning with that belief.

The Universe Supports Your Expansion

The intelligence that moves through all things is not indifferent to your desires. It wants to experience itself more fully through you. It wants you to have the tools, the resources, and the opportunities that will allow you to live your highest expression. It is not selfish to desire more—it is the natural impulse of life itself.

But remember, life expands not only through receiving but through giving. As you increase, so should your capacity to uplift others. True wealth is never about hoarding—it is about circulating abundance, allowing it to flow through you and into the world.

The Path Forward

The only thing that can limit your wealth is your own doubt. The moment you hesitate, the moment you question whether abundance is truly available to you, you create resistance. But when you step fully into the knowing that riches are already on their way to you, everything shifts.

You do not need to worry about competition. You do not need to fear that others are "getting there first." What is meant for you cannot be taken away, and the universe has limitless ways of bringing it to you.

All that is required is your unwavering faith, your alignment with the creative force, and your willingness to act from a place of certainty. Riches are not something you must chase—they are something you allow.

SEVEN

GRATITUDE

"The real gift of gratitude is that the more grateful you are, the more present you become."

— Robert Holden

The first step toward receiving abundance is aligning yourself with the intelligence that creates all things. This alignment does not require effort, struggle, or competition. It requires something far simpler—gratitude.

Gratitude is the key that unlocks the flow of abundance. It is not merely a polite response to receiving what you desire; it is the very state of being that allows you to receive more. When you live in gratitude, you are in harmony with the source of all creation. You recognize that life itself is constantly giving, and in turn, you open yourself to receive.

Gratitude and the Flow of Life

Despite working hard and making wise choices, many people remain in struggle because they are disconnected from gratitude. They focus on what is missing, what is lacking, and what has not yet arrived. In doing so, they reinforce their sense of lack and close themselves off from the abundance waiting to flow to them.

Gratitude, on the other hand, brings you into immediate harmony with the creative energy of the universe. When you express gratitude for what you already have, you acknowledge the infinite nature of supply. You say to life, "I see what you have given, and I trust that more is always on the way."

This is not a technique to manipulate reality—it is an acknowledgment of what is already true. The more you appreciate what is, the more you align with what is coming. Life moves toward those who recognize its gifts, just as the sun rises to meet the open sky.

The Law of Gratitude

The energy you send out returns to you. When you radiate gratitude, you create an irresistible pull toward more of what you are grateful for. This is the natural flow of existence. You cannot receive abundance while holding thoughts of dissatisfaction, resentment, or fear. The two states cannot coexist. To dwell in gratitude is to dwell in expansion, trust, and certainty that all is well and will continue to be well.

Shifting from Lack to Abundance

If you find yourself caught in a cycle of focusing on what is missing, shift your awareness. Look around you and recognize even the smallest blessings. The air you breathe, the food you eat, the opportunities already present in your life are signs that the universe is already providing for you.

When you focus on these gifts, your mind begins to expect more. Expectation becomes faith. Faith dissolves doubt. And in this space of trust, the channels of abundance open wide.

Gratitude Transforms Your Reality

A person who cultivates gratitude does not dwell on limitations. They do not concern themselves with competition, nor do they feel threatened by the wealth of others. They know that life's abundance is infinite and that their good cannot be taken from them.

Likewise, gratitude prevents the mind from sinking into dissatisfaction. To dwell on what is wrong is to create more of what is wrong. To dwell on what is good is to multiply goodness.

This is not about ignoring challenges but about choosing your focus. Challenges exist, but so does opportunity. In every difficulty, there is potential for growth. When you see life through the lens of gratitude, even obstacles become stepping stones to greater abundance.

The Energy of Gratitude Creates Faith

Faith is not blind belief. It is the natural byproduct of a grateful mind. When you trust in life's abundance, you do not need to force faith—it arises effortlessly. Each moment of gratitude strengthens this trust, making it easier to believe that more is always on the way.

Gratitude Must Be Continuous

This is not a practice to engage in only when things are going well. It must be a continuous way of being. Every moment holds something to appreciate, and every situation, no matter how it appears, holds the potential for good.

Even those who seem to work against you are part of the unfolding process. There is no need to resist or resent. The world is arranging itself for your benefit, whether you perceive it in the moment or not. By holding gratitude for all things—including the lessons disguised as struggles—you remain in harmony with the greater flow of life.

Becoming a Magnet for Goodness

To be grateful is to align with the fundamental truth of existence: life is abundant. When you embody this truth, you naturally attract more of it. You do not need to chase success or struggle for wealth. You simply need to remain in harmony with the intelligence that is always seeking to express more through you.

The path is simple: give thanks, expect good, and know that all you desire is already moving toward you. In this state of gratitude, abundance becomes inevitable.

EIGHT

THINKING IN THE CERTAIN WAY

"Whether you think you can, or you think you can't—you're right."

— Henry Ford

Clarity is power. If you wish to bring something into your life, you must first imagine it clearly and distinctly. Vague wishes and scattered desires create nothing; only a focused, unwavering vision can shape reality.

Many people do not receive what they seek because their thoughts are unfocused. They hold conflicting desires, shift between desires, and never commit to a single, definite vision. The universe does not respond to uncertainty—it responds to clarity, precision, and an unwavering intention. Before you can receive, you must know exactly what you seek.

The Power of a Definite Vision

Imagine a sailor navigating the ocean. He does not drift aimlessly, hoping the wind will carry him somewhere desirable. He sets his course, keeps his eyes on the horizon, and adjusts his actions to stay aligned with his destination. Your thoughts must work in the same way. Fix your mind on your vision as a sailor fixes his gaze on the compass, refusing to be distracted by momentary waves or changing winds.

You do not need elaborate rituals, lengthy affirmations, or mystical exercises to manifest what you desire. You need only to be certain. When a vision is deeply held, it remains effortlessly in your awareness. You will not need to force yourself to think about it; it will be as present in your mind as the air you breathe.

The Role of Desire and Commitment

The depth of your desire determines the strength of your focus. Your mind will wander if you are only mildly interested in achieving wealth. But if your desire is strong—if it arises from a deep recognition that your expansion is part of the natural flow of life—then your thoughts will remain centered on it with ease.

Your desire must be greater than your tendency toward mental laziness. If you wish for wealth but are unwilling to consistently direct your thoughts toward that goal, your wish will remain a passing thought, not a creative force. Those who achieve wealth do not do so by chance but by holding their vision with unwavering certainty.

More Than Just Visualization

Seeing your vision clearly is only the beginning. If visualization alone were enough, the world would be full of dreamers who never act. The true power comes when you combine your vision with purpose and faith.

- **Purpose:** You must not only see the vision—you must commit to making it real. This commitment fuels action, guiding you toward the decisions and opportunities that will bring your vision into reality.

- **Faith:** With absolute certainty, you must believe that what you seek is already yours in the unseen realm and is now making its way into form.

Live as if you are already in possession of what you seek. If you desire a new home, begin to feel what it is like to live in that home. If you seek financial freedom, adopt the mindset of someone who is already free. The mental state of ownership precedes the physical reality of possession.

Gratitude Strengthens Faith

To hold your vision unwaveringly, practice gratitude. Be as thankful for the things you desire as you are for the things you already have. Gratitude signals to the universe that you are in alignment with abundance and that you trust the process of creation.

When you express gratitude in advance, you affirm that your desire is already on its way to you. This deepens your faith and removes doubt, which is the only force that can disrupt the manifestation process.

Prayer Without Ceasing

Prayer is not about repeating requests to the universe—but about living in a state of belief. The moment you have formed a clear vision and impressed it upon the unseen intelligence of life, your task is not to keep asking but to keep receiving.

This means acting, thinking, and speaking as though what you desire is already a part of your reality. Do not wish for it—

claim it. Do not hope for it—expect it. Live with the certainty that the unseen forces of creation are working on your behalf.

The Difference Between a Dreamer and a Creator

A dreamer sees a beautiful vision and wishes for it. A creator holds the vision, believes in its reality, and acts upon it. Faith and purpose transform imagination into manifestation. The difference between a dreamer and a creator is the unwavering certainty that what is held in mind will soon be held in hand.

To think in the Certain Way is to refuse doubt, to reject limitation, and to stand firm in the knowing that your vision is as real now as it will be when it takes physical form. This is not merely positive thinking but the application of an eternal law.

Know what you desire. Hold your vision with clarity. Act in faith. Express gratitude. Move forward without hesitation. In doing so, you align with the infinite creative force of life, and what you seek cannot help but move toward you.

NINE

How to Use the Will

"Self-discipline begins with the mastery of your thoughts. If you don't control what you think, you can't control what you do."

— Napoleon Hill

The power of your will is not meant to be exerted over others or external circumstances. True power lies in mastering yourself.

To use your will effectively in creating wealth, you must direct it inward—to discipline your thoughts, to sustain your vision, and to keep yourself aligned with the certain way of thinking. The purpose of your will is not to force external events to bend to your desires but to keep your mind unwaveringly fixed upon what you seek.

The Misuse of Willpower

Many people believe that getting rich requires the forceful exertion of will over others, manipulating circumstances, or competing ruthlessly. This is an illusion. Attempting to control others—whether by physical coercion or mental influence—is a misunderstanding of how life works. The universe does not respond to force; it responds to alignment.

You do not need to impose your will upon others to have what you desire. The creative process does not require struggle or competition. Wealth does not come by seizing what belongs to someone else but by bringing new creations into being.

Directing Your Will Where It Matters

The only place where willpower is truly effective is within yourself. Use it to command your attention, to discipline your thoughts, and to prevent doubt or fear from taking hold. Your will must be used to keep your mind focused on abundance, not scarcity; on creation, not competition; on certainty, not hesitation.

Faith is the key to creation, and your will is the tool that holds faith in place. If you allow yourself to waver, to entertain doubt, or to focus on limitations, you will interrupt the creative process. The power of your will is to keep your mind aligned with truth, regardless of external appearances.

The Energy of Focused Thought

Every thought you hold with faith and certainty influences the unseen forces of creation. The universe responds not to force but to certainty. When your thoughts are held steadily in a state of belief, they radiate outward and initiate unseen movements that draw your desires into reality.

Most people make the mistake of allowing negative thoughts to creep in—fear, worry, and doubt. These thoughts create countercurrents, pushing away the very things they seek.

Each moment spent in fear moves your desires further away, just as each moment spent in faith moves them closer.

The Will to Avoid Negative Influence

Your environment, the media, and even well-meaning people may constantly remind you of lack, struggle, and competition. If you allow these influences to dominate your thinking, they will shape your reality. This is where your will must be strongest.

Do not dwell on poverty or suffering because what you focus on expands. Do not spend time analyzing economic inequality, the limitations of the world, or the struggles of others. This does not mean you are indifferent—it means you refuse to let images of lack shape your mind.

If you wish to uplift others, do not focus on their suffering—focus on their potential. You do not help the poor by thinking of poverty; you help them by demonstrating abundance. Show them, by your success, that wealth is possible for all.

The Difference Between Creation and Competition

Competition is based on the belief that resources are limited, and that one must fight for a share. But creation recognizes that wealth is infinite. The universe has no shortage of ideas, opportunities, or resources. The more you create, the more you add to the world. When you create wealth, you do not take from another—you open a path for others to follow.

Every person who becomes rich through competition leaves behind barriers for others. But every person who becomes rich through creation leaves behind inspiration and opportunity. Your success does not reduce the success of others; it expands the realm of possibility for all.

The Power of Absolute Focus

Your greatest asset is your ability to hold a vision unwaveringly. When you focus your will upon your vision and refuse to be distracted by fear, external conditions, or the doubts of others, you become unstoppable.

Your will is not to force things into being but to maintain a steady faith, unwavering purpose, and alignment with the creative power that governs all things.

Hold your vision. Use your will to reject doubt. Know with certainty that what you desire is already moving toward you. This is the true use of willpower—the ability to stay aligned with your highest vision until it becomes reality.

TEN

Further Use of the Will

"You cannot swim for new horizons until you have courage to lose sight of the shore."

— William Faulkner

Your mind is a powerful instrument. To harness its true potential, you must learn to direct it with intention. Creating wealth is not about efforting, forcing, or struggling—it is about maintaining an unshakable vision while refusing to entertain opposing ideas. Your ability to hold this vision is what determines your success.

Let Go of the Past

Many people sabotage their future by continually revisiting the past. Dwelling on former struggles, financial hardships, or the limitations of one's upbringing only reinforces those patterns. The mind tends to recreate what it focuses on; if you continually reflect on lack, you will bring more of it into your experience.

Let the past dissolve. It has no power unless you give it attention. Your future wealth is not dependent on your past experiences but on your present thoughts and actions. As Jesus said, "Let the dead bury their dead." Your only concern is the abundant life ahead of you.

Align with Growth, Not Decay

Countless theories describe a world in decline, a society in chaos, and an economy in collapse. These perspectives are illusions. The world is not falling apart—it is evolving, expanding, and moving toward greater abundance.

If you direct your attention toward failure, struggle, and decline, you will find evidence of it everywhere. But if you focus on progress, opportunity, and expansion, you will see that the world is moving toward ever-greater wealth. The truth is that the universe is inherently abundant, and life continually seeks to express more of itself through you.

The Law of Focus

You cannot dwell on poverty and create riches. You cannot study limitation and expect to experience abundance. What you focus on expands. If you wish to grow rich, you must focus only on the idea of wealth, expansion, and unlimited potential.

When you speak of the poor, see them as those who are becoming rich. When you observe your financial situation, focus on what is growing, not on what is lacking. The energy you send into the world comes back to you multiplied—so choose to send out thoughts of abundance.

Wealth is a Noble Aim

Some may think that pursuing wealth is selfish or materialistic. This is a misunderstanding. True wealth is not about hoarding resources—it is about creating and contributing. The greatest acts of service and the most profound advancements in science, art, and human well-being have all come from those with the resources to express their highest potential.

When you become rich through creation—not competition—you uplift others. You set an example that abundance is possible for all. You become a source of inspiration, not pity. Your success is not just for you; it is for the expansion of life itself.

Protect Your Mind from Contradictory Influences

Your mental environment is as important as your physical one. Be selective about what you consume—whether it be books, news, conversations, or ideas.

Do not immerse yourself in stories of poverty, struggle, or decline. This does not mean you ignore the suffering in the world—it means you choose to focus on solutions rather than problems. The greatest way to help others is not by lamenting their hardships but by showing them the path to abundance through your example.

The Best Service You Can Offer

The poor do not need charity; they need inspiration. A loaf of bread feeds them for a moment, but a vision of possibility feeds them for a lifetime. Your responsibility is not to fix the world's problems but to demonstrate what is possible. When you live abundantly, others are drawn toward that same path.

The greatest service you can render is to become the fullest expression of yourself. When you step into your power, you naturally uplift those around you. You teach by being, not by struggling. This is the highest form of contribution.

The Importance of Mental Clarity

There are many philosophies, theories, and teachings about wealth and success. But truth is simple. Just as mathematics has one fundamental system of computation, the principles of wealth creation are direct and clear. Avoid overcomplicating the process.

Focus on the principles that lead directly to success:

- Hold a clear and unwavering vision of what you desire.
- Refuse to entertain contradictory thoughts or beliefs.
- Maintain faith that what you seek is already on its way to you.
- Act in alignment with the abundant nature of the universe.

If you find yourself confused or uncertain, simplify. Return to these core truths. Do not allow conflicting ideas to distract you. Stay on the path with absolute certainty.

Final Thoughts

Your mind is the most powerful tool you possess. Direct it wisely. Let go of past limitations, ignore narratives of decline, and focus entirely on the vision of what you are creating. The world is not in chaos—it is in evolution. Wealth is not scarce—it is infinite. Your success does not take from others—it opens doors for them.

Live fully, think abundantly, and act decisively. In doing so, you step into your true nature as a creator, and the world will reshape itself to match your vision.

ELEVEN

ACTING IN THE CERTAIN WAY

"The way to get started is to quit talking and begin doing."

— Walt Disney

Thought is the foundation of creation, but it is not enough on its own. Thought, no matter how powerful, must be accompanied by action. To live in alignment with abundance, you must move beyond passive contemplation and step into active participation with life. Many people who understand the principles of abundance falter here—they think without acting, blocking the flow of what is trying to reach them.

The Fusion of Thought and Action

You are not required to force events into place. Your task is to align your thoughts with certainty, to hold a clear vision, and to take action in the present moment. The movement of the universe is always bringing opportunities your way, but you must be in a position to receive them. The gold in the mountains does not mine itself; the doors that open must be walked through.

You do not control the process by which your desires are fulfilled. The unseen intelligence of life coordinates that. Your role is to act in faith, recognize opportunities when they arrive, and move toward your vision.

The Time to Act is Now

You cannot act in the past, for it is gone. You cannot act in the future, for it has not yet come. You can only act now. This is the only place where creation happens. Many people delay taking action, waiting for the "perfect conditions" or a "better time." But waiting is a form of resistance—it is a declaration that you do not yet believe in the certainty of your vision.

If you think you must change your environment or circumstances before you can begin, you are mistaken. Begin now. Act where you are. Your actions today will naturally move you toward better circumstances. The external world will shift in response to the energy of your decisive movement.

Do Not Wait for Opportunities—Create Them

Some people believe they must first obtain the perfect job, the perfect business, or the perfect situation before they can act. But it is not the external that changes first—it is the internal. Hold the vision of your desire, but engage fully with what is in front of you. Your current job, business, or environment is the stepping stone to the next.

If you are not in the business or situation you desire, do not resist where you are. Use it as a tool to transition to where you want to be. Align your thinking with the life you want, and take purposeful action within the life you have now. The unseen intelligence of the universe will bridge the gap for you.

Focus on Present Action, Not Future Worries

Many people get lost in contemplating future scenarios—trying to predict what will happen, analyzing every possibility, or worrying about what might go wrong. This creates paralysis. The mind is divided between present action and imagined fears, reducing the effectiveness of both.

Trust that you will meet future circumstances with the wisdom required at the time. Focus entirely on what can be done now. The most powerful force in creation is undivided attention in the present moment.

The Illusion of Magical Thinking

Do not mistake creative thought for magical thinking. The process of creation is not about sitting idly, expecting wealth to materialize without movement. You are not required to force events, but you are required to participate. Your thoughts set the process in motion, but your actions guide it into form. Thought brings opportunities; action secures them.

The Power of Acting with Certainty

Action must be taken with the same certainty you hold in your mind. Move forward as if your vision is already materializing. When you act this way, you become a magnet for opportunities, success, and everything that aligns with your beliefs. The world responds to the energy of conviction.

Hold Your Vision and Take Action

As you step forward, hold your vision firmly in mind. Do not entertain doubt. Do not wait for circumstances to change before you move. Act now, where you are, with what you have, and watch as life arranges itself around your certainty.

This is the bridge between thought and reality—this is acting in the Certain Way.

TWELVE

Efficient Action

"Perfection is not attainable, but if we chase perfection we can catch excellence."

— Vince Lombardi

Your thoughts are the foundation of creation, but thought alone is not enough. You must act, and more importantly, you must act efficiently. Many fail because they separate thought from action, believing mental vision alone will bring results. However, the universe responds not only to intention but also to movement.

The Principle of Efficient Action

You can only advance by exceeding your current place. The world evolves because those who succeed do more than what is expected of them. Growth occurs when you outgrow your current limitations, expanding beyond them into new levels of success.

If every person fell short of their present capacity, progress would halt, and life would regress. Nature itself advances through the principle of excess energy—when life has more energy than it needs, it evolves into higher forms. The same is true for you.

The key to getting rich is applying this principle to your actions. Each day is either a step forward or a missed opportunity. If you fail to do what can be done today, you delay your progress indefinitely. A single neglected action could mean a missed opportunity that would have set powerful forces in motion.

Act Fully, But Without Strain

A common misconception is that success comes from working harder and doing more. This is not true. Wealth comes not from the number of things you do but from the *efficiency* of each action.

Do not confuse busyness with productivity. Many exhaust themselves by doing countless ineffective tasks, believing that sheer effort will bring results. One powerful, intentional action is worth more than a hundred weak, distracted ones.

Your goal is not to do more but to do *each thing in the most effective way possible*. Every action you take should be strong, deliberate, and infused with faith and purpose.

Thought and Action Must Be One

Many fail because they separate their mental power from their actions. They visualize wealth but take action without presence, focus, or alignment. Their thoughts move in one direction while their actions move in another, creating inefficiency and delay.

Success comes when every action is infused with the full power of your vision. When thought and action become one, the smallest task becomes a step toward your greater goal. When done with full presence, each act opens the way for the next and the next, creating a momentum of success that cannot be stopped.

Progress Is Cumulative

Every act done in an efficient manner builds upon the last. As you move toward your vision, new opportunities, new people, and new resources will be drawn to you. Your influence will expand, and life will respond with greater abundance.

Each day, do *all* that you can do within that day. But do not try to do tomorrow's work today. Act fully in the present moment, with your mind engaged in what you are doing now. The present is where creation happens.

How to Hold the Vision While Acting

As you work, keep your mental picture alive. You do not need to constantly focus on the small details—those must be contemplated in moments of stillness. Instead, let your vision remain in the background of your awareness, subtly guiding your actions.

This is how you bring the full force of your creative energy into every moment. As you hold your vision, you will act with greater clarity, efficiency, and purpose. Your energy will be strong, and each action will be infused with power.

The Formula for Efficient Action

Hold a clear vision of what you want.

1. Move beyond your current limitations by exceeding what is required of you.

2. Do every action with full presence, faith, and purpose.

3. Avoid inefficiency—focus on the quality, not the quantity, of your actions.

4. Trust that the right opportunities will come from your aligned action.

5. Each day, do all that can be done in that day—but without force or strain.

By following this process, you align yourself with the natural laws of growth and abundance. You begin to move with life rather than against it. And as you take each step, life will respond, bringing you exactly what you need at the perfect time.

This is how success unfolds—not through struggle, but through alignment.

THIRTEEN

GETTING INTO THE RIGHT BUSINESS

"If you don't build your dream, someone else will hire you to help them build theirs."

— Tony Gaskins

Success in any field depends not only on skill but on alignment with your inner purpose. Your faculties—whether in music, mechanics, commerce, or any other field—are merely tools. Tools alone do not create success. The way you use them and the consciousness you bring to them determines the outcome.

Many skilled musicians, artisans, and merchants never achieve wealth. Talent is not enough; you must also apply your abilities in the right way. Just as two carpenters can use the same tools yet produce work of vastly different quality, so too can two people with the same faculties create completely different results based on how they engage with their work.

The Business That Fits You

Generally, you will find success most easily in a business that allows you to express your strongest abilities. However, your present skills do not define your potential. You are not limited by the talents you were born with. Growth is always possible; any skill can be developed with intention and practice.

The best business for you is the one you are most naturally suited for and the one you deeply desire to pursue. Desire is an indication of potential. When you feel drawn to a particular field, it is because the power to succeed in it is already within you, waiting to be cultivated.

Desire as a Manifestation of Potential

The longing to play music is evidence that the ability to play music exists within you, waiting for expression. The desire to create, innovate, and lead—all these impulses point toward latent abilities that can be developed.

If you have a strong desire to engage in a particular type of work, it means that the capacity to succeed in that work is within you. It may be dormant, but it is there, waiting to be awakened through practice and dedication.

Moving Toward Your Right Vocation

If you find yourself in a job or business that does not align with your true desires, do not act impulsively to escape it. The best way to transition into your true calling is through *gradual growth*.

However, if a clear and aligned opportunity arises, and you feel a deep certainty that it is the right move, do not hesitate. True opportunities come not through fear or desperation but through a deep sense of knowing. When you are in doubt, wait. Spend time in stillness, contemplating your vision. The right decision will become apparent when you align with gratitude and trust.

There Is No Competition, Only Creation

You are not in a race against others. When you shift from a mindset of competition to one of creation, you will see that there is no scarcity. If one opportunity passes, another will appear. The universe is abundant, and there is space for everyone's success.

When you hurry, you step into the energy of fear. Fear creates resistance. Whenever you feel rushed or anxious, pause. Return to your vision. Cultivate gratitude for what is already unfolding. In stillness, clarity emerges.

The Power of Gratitude

Gratitude aligns you with abundance. When you feel uncertain, step back into a state of appreciation. Recognize that your path is unfolding perfectly, and trust that the right opportunities will appear at the right time.

Mistakes happen when you act from fear, doubt, or impatience. But when you act from a place of deep faith and purpose, every step you take will be the right one.

Aligning with the Flow of Life

1. Pursue the work you deeply desire, for desire signals latent potential.

2. If you are not in the right vocation, use your current situation as a stepping stone toward what you truly want.

3. Do not act out of haste or fear; wait for the right mo-

ment with deep faith.

4.   Recognize that opportunities are limitless—there is no competition, only creation.

5.   Gratitude strengthens faith and aligns you with the abundance already moving toward you.

The right business for you is the one that allows you to express who you truly are. Move toward it with trust, knowing that life guides you to the perfect opportunity.

FOURTEEN

THE IMPRESSION OF INCREASE

"To give without any reward, or any notice, has a special quality of its own."

— Anne Morrow Lindbergh

Wherever you are, whatever you do, recognize that life itself is always expanding. It does not shrink. It does not contract. It moves in the direction of more—more expression, more being, more life. This is not a belief to be adopted but an observable truth. Everything in existence is either growing or dissolving. Nothing remains static.

You are part of this movement of life, and so is everyone you encounter. In every interaction, whether personal or professional, you contribute to expansion or reinforce limitation. To truly embody the science of getting rich, you must consciously align with this law of increase.

It does not matter if you are in the ideal business or wish to transition into something new. What matters is how you are in this moment—how you engage with what is before you.

Expansion does not come from rejection of where you are but from full presence and mastery in your current situation.

You may wish to move into a different profession, but the way to do so is not through struggle or impatience. You transition into something greater by embodying greatness where you stand now.

Becoming a Source of Increase

Everyone you meet, every person you serve, is seeking increase—whether they know it or not. They may not call it that, but they want more life, fulfillment, and meaning. And because you understand this law, you can give it to them—not through material goods alone, but through the energy and consciousness you bring to every interaction.

Whatever you offer—a product, a service, or a conversation—let it contain the energy of increase. Let people leave your presence feeling expanded, not diminished. When someone does business with you, let them feel they have gained something beyond what they paid for. Even if they buy only a simple item from you, let them walk away with a sense that their life is now richer.

This does not require clever words or persuasive tactics. It requires only that you hold the deep, unshakable conviction that you are a source of increase and that every person who crosses your path is uplifted by their connection to you.

The Power of Silent Assurance

True power does not seek validation. It does not boast or proclaim itself. When you are aligned with the principle of increase, others will sense it in you without a word needing to be spoken.

The person who brags about their wealth, success, or status reveals their own inner lack. They are still identified with the competitive mind, where one must prove superiority over others. This is not the way of true wealth.

Instead, be still within yourself. Move through the world with quiet assurance. When people interact with you, let them feel something intangible but undeniable—a presence that reassures them, a sense of possibility, a feeling that they, too, are moving toward greater life.

When you operate from this space, people will be drawn to you, not out of obligation or manipulation, but because they instinctively recognize that their expansion is linked to your presence.

Increase, Not Control

Beware of the subtle temptation to seek power over others. Many people desire influence not to serve but to dominate. This is the way of kings and rulers, of those who believe that wealth is a game of taking rather than creating. It is the path of struggle, not abundance.

To seek mastery over others is to align with fear, limitation, and lack. The creative mind does not need to control others or prove its worth. It simply aligns with the flow of life and, in doing so, naturally rises.

Let your only desire be to give more life—not to dictate, not to manipulate, not to be above others, but to be a channel through which increase flows to all.

As you align with this law of increase, you will see that wealth is not something you pursue. It is something that moves toward you. It is not something you must struggle for; it is something that unfolds naturally when you stop resisting the flow of life.

The Certain Way

Hold to your vision. Know that the more you embody the principle of increase, the more the universe will align to bring you what you need. Every step you take in this state of certainty moves you closer to your goal—not because you are forcing it, but because you are in harmony with how life operates.

And so, as you go about your work, do not worry. Do not rush. Do not seek to control. Simply become a presence of increase, and life will respond in kind.

What you want for yourself, you must also want for all.

This is the secret. This is the law. This is the way.

FIFTEEN

THE ADVANCING MAN

"We cannot become what we need to
be by remaining what we are."

— John C. Maxwell

Regardless of your profession—whether you are a doctor, a teacher, a laborer, or an artist—the principle remains the same: if you become a source of increase, life will expand for you. This is not about manipulating circumstances or struggling for a position; it is about aligning yourself with the ever-unfolding nature of life itself.

The physician who clearly and unwaveringly envisions himself as a healer, who does not merely diagnose symptoms but sees his work as an act of expansion and wholeness, will naturally draw more people toward him. Healing is not just in the method but in the energy behind it. When a doctor embodies a consciousness of abundance, patients will feel it. They will sense that there is more life in his presence, not just the absence of illness.

The same is true for the teacher who does not simply transfer knowledge but inspires a thirst for learning. The preacher who does not merely recite doctrine but awakens a sense of divine connection in others. The lawyer who does not merely argue cases but sees his work as the restoration of harmony and justice.

Whatever field you are in, if you hold a vision of yourself as a force of increase, as someone through whom life expresses itself in ever greater ways, you will not lack opportunities. People gravitate toward those who expand their sense of what is possible.

Beyond the Workplace

The advancing man is not simply looking for promotion, recognition, or financial gain. He is not concerned with currying favor with an employer or hoping that someone else will grant him advancement. By his very nature, he is too large for his current position—not in the sense of arrogance, but in the quiet knowing that he is continuously expanding.

If there seems to be no room for advancement where you are, do not immediately concern yourself with changing your job. Concern yourself first with changing your consciousness. The world will shift around you as a reflection of your inner state. New opportunities will appear when your expansion becomes undeniable—not because you searched for them desperately, but because they must.

The Power That Moves You

You are not working alone. The same intelligence that causes a tree to grow toward the sun, that causes the tides to move in rhythm with the moon, is working within you. It responds to the certainty of your purpose. It aligns circumstances to match your inner state.

If you hold firm to your vision—without doubt, without wavering—the opportunities you need will arise. You do not have to beg, plead, or manipulate. You simply have to align yourself with the principle of expansion.

When you act with unwavering faith and purpose, people feel it. Your presence alone becomes magnetic. Without seeking control over others, without striving for dominance, you will naturally rise. The old way—the competitive mind— believes that success comes through struggle, through overpowering others. But the advancing man knows that true success comes by being in harmony with the movement of life itself.

No One Can Hold You Back

There is nothing in your present situation that can limit you unless you believe that it can. No external force—not your employer, not the economy, not societal structures—has the power to suppress the life that is moving through you.

If you are in a job where you feel stuck, understand this: the moment you begin to embody the principle of increase, the moment you stop seeing yourself as limited by circumstances, new doors will open.

The steel trust, or any corporate structure, can only keep people in conditions of limitation so long as those people do not understand their own power. The moment they do, the system must change. Life does not allow stagnation. The creative force always moves toward greater freedom and greater possibility.

The advancing man does not wait. He acts now. He does not wait for the perfect opportunity to arrive; he makes himself so expansive, so full of purpose, that opportunity must find him.

The First Step is Enough

You may not see the entire path ahead. That is not your concern. The way forward is revealed as you walk. When an opportunity arises—even if it is not the final destination—take it. Life is not static. One step leads to another, and soon, you will find yourself in a place you could not have imagined from where you started.

There is no scarcity of opportunity. The only scarcity exists in the minds of those who believe in limitation. The universe is structured to support expansion. It cannot be otherwise.

The Certainty of Increase

Let this be your foundation:

1. There is a universal intelligence that moves all things toward greater life.

2. You are an expression of this intelligence, and your life expands as you align with it.

3. Your work—whatever it is—is an opportunity to embody the principle of increase.

4. You will naturally rise by holding a clear vision, acting with certainty, and embodying the energy of growth.

5. Opportunities are not something you chase; they appear in response to your state of being.

The advancing man does not hope, does not wish, and does not doubt. He simply *is*. He moves forward with the quiet, unshakable, knowing that life is always working for him, never against him.

We'd Love to Hear From You!

Thank you so much for reading this book-it means the world to me. If you found it helpful, inspiring, or just enjoyable, would you take a moment to leave a review? Your feedback not only helps others but also keeps me motivated to create more valuable content for you.

Here's how you can leave a review:

1. Scan the QR code on this page to go directly to the author's page.

2. Or, visit your Amazon Orders page, find this book, and click "Write a Product Review."

Your kind words make a big difference.
Thank you for your support!

SIXTEEN

SOME CAUTIONS AND CONCLUDING OBSERVATIONS

"Nothing in the world can take the place of persistence...Persistence and determination alone are omnipotent."

— Calvin Coolidge

Many dismiss the idea that there is a precise science to getting rich. They believe wealth is a fixed quantity that can only be distributed, not created. They insist that social and political structures must change before abundance can be accessible to all. But this is a fundamental misunderstanding of how reality unfolds.

Systems of government, business, and industry have indeed created structures that appear to limit wealth. However, those structures exist only because people have accepted them as reality. They are not absolute; they shift when enough people begin to think and act differently. The system does not control the individual; it is the collective consciousness of individuals that shapes the system.

If enough people awaken to the truth that abundance is not scarce but infinite, that it is a natural expression of life itself, then no institution, economic model, or government policy can keep them in poverty. Change begins at the level of thought, not at the level of policy.

Moving Beyond Competition

The old way—the competitive mind—sees wealth as something to be taken, something that can be hoarded or lost. It sees success as a struggle, an effort to get ahead at someone else's expense. But the creative mind knows otherwise.

The more people who get rich through competition, the worse off the world becomes. Wealth gained through competition creates fear, division, and imbalance. But the more people who get rich through creative thought, the more wealth there is for everyone. When one person becomes truly rich—through expansion, through alignment with life—they uplift others. They create opportunities. They inspire. They make new possibilities visible.

The world's economic salvation will not come from redistribution or overthrowing the existing systems. It will come from a large number of individuals practicing the principles laid out in this book. When enough people do this, society's structures will transform to accommodate the new reality.

For now, it is enough to know that no external system can keep you from abundance. You do not belong to an economic class or a social category. Your circumstances do not define you.

You are not at the mercy of the market, the government, or the decisions of others.

The moment you think in the Certain Way—holding a vision of increase, moving with faith and purpose—you rise above all limitations. You become a citizen of another reality.

Let Go of Fear

Your greatest enemy is doubt. The moment you begin to question whether there is enough, whether the opportunity is real, or whether forces beyond your control might block your path, you disconnect from the creative flow.

There is no lack. There is no opposing force trying to keep you small. There is only the movement of life and your willingness to align with it.

Do not waste energy worrying about the future. Do not ask, "What if things go wrong? What if obstacles arise?" No obstruction can stop you if you act in harmony with the creative process. Whatever appears as a roadblock will dissolve as you approach it. Or you will find a way over it. Or around it.

If you keep moving in the Certain Way, the path will always reveal itself.

Speak Only in Terms of Growth

Be mindful of your words.

Never speak of yourself, your work, or your life in a way that implies limitation. Do not declare that times are hard, lament difficult circumstances, or engage in conversations that reinforce scarcity.

The world may appear chaotic, but appearances do not bind you. Others may struggle because they believe struggle is inevitable. You do not have to participate in that belief.

If you hold steady to the truth that wealth and expansion are your birthright, you will find that what seems like difficult times for others will be your greatest period of growth. When others are retreating in fear, you will be advancing with confidence.

Your words shape your world. Speak only in terms of expansion. See everything as becoming, unfolding, and moving toward a greater life. Even what appears as failure is not failure—it is simply life redirecting you toward something better.

Disappointment is an Illusion

There may be moments when things do not happen as quickly as expected. You may have envisioned a certain opportunity unfolding in a specific way, only to see it vanish. But understand this: life is never withholding from you. If something does not manifest as you expected, it is because something greater is already in motion.

A man once pursued a business deal with all his energy, convinced that it was the key to his success. But at the last moment, it fell apart. He did not see this as failure. He did not sink into disappointment. He remained in gratitude, trusting that if this deal had not happened, there was a reason.

Not long after, a far greater opportunity appeared—one he could not have foreseen. He might have missed it if he had been trapped in the energy of disappointment.

This is how it works. If something does not happen, it is only because a larger, more aligned reality is forming. Trust it. Move forward.

Ability Will Meet You on the Path

Some hesitate because they believe they lack the skill, the knowledge, or the ability to succeed. They wait until they feel "ready." But readiness does not come first. Readiness comes as you move.

If you are aligned with your vision, the ability to meet each challenge will arise exactly when you need it. This is not wishful thinking; it is how life unfolds. The mind that creates the vision also provides the means to fulfill it.

Abraham Lincoln was an uneducated man. He had no formal training, political background, wealth, or influence. And yet, when he stepped onto the path, the ability to lead an entire nation through its greatest crisis emerged within him. That same intelligence is available to you.

You do not have to know how you will do something before you begin. You only have to begin. The next step will always appear.

Protect Your Mind

This book contains everything you need to know about the science of getting rich. Until these ideas are fully anchored in your consciousness, be careful what influences you allow into your mind.

Avoid literature, conversations, and environments that reinforce the old scarcity paradigm. Do not engage in arguments about economic conditions, competition, or the impossibility of wealth. You are moving beyond those things.

Spend your time contemplating your vision. Cultivate gratitude. Align yourself with the feeling of already having what you desire. Do not allow conflicting beliefs to take root in your mind.

Once you have mastered this way of thinking, you will no longer need to shield yourself. You will be so firmly grounded in abundance that no external idea can shake you. Until then, be mindful.

The Final Truth

Let this be your foundation:

- External conditions do not bind you. The world shifts as your mind shifts.

- There is no scarcity, only expansion. When you align with expansion, life moves to support you.

- No obstacle is permanent. Every challenge carries the seed of its own solution.

- Failure does not exist. There is only redirection toward something greater.

- You do not need to know how everything will unfold. You only need to take the next step.

If you live in this way and act with unwavering faith and purpose, you cannot fail. The laws that govern wealth are as precise as the laws of mathematics.

Move forward with certainty. The path will unfold beneath your feet.

SEVENTEEN

SUMMARY OF THE NEW SCIENCE OF GETTING RICH

"Act as if what you do makes a difference. It does."

—William James

There is an invisible intelligence that pervades all things—a formless, creative presence that is the foundation of everything that exists. It is the space between thoughts, the stillness beyond form, the field of infinite potential. It moves in accordance with the impressions made upon it by thought.

A thought, clearly held and deeply felt, is an instruction to this formless intelligence. It is an energetic blueprint, a pattern that the universe responds to.

You are not separate from this intelligence. You are not an isolated being struggling to survive in a hostile world. You are an expression of the One Life, connected to the whole. And because you are connected, you have the power to shape your reality.

You do this not by competing, not by grasping, not by striving—but by aligning with the creative flow of life itself.

Moving from Competition to Creation

The world has taught you that success is about competition, about taking your share before someone else does. But this is an illusion. The more you think in terms of competition, the more you reinforce the belief that resources are limited, that you must struggle to get ahead, and that you are separate from the source of abundance.

The creative mind knows there is no scarcity. There is only expansion. There is only becoming. When you shift from competition to creation, you step into harmony with the infinite intelligence that sustains all things.

The Power of Gratitude

Gratitude is not a polite gesture. It is not an obligation. It is a state of being that aligns you with the creative forces of the universe. When you feel gratitude—not as a fleeting thought but as a deep and abiding presence—you open yourself to receiving.

You do not need to beg or plead. You do not need to prove yourself worthy. The moment you are truly grateful, you are already in harmony with abundance—gratitude bridges where you are and where you want to be.

To remain on the creative plane, cultivate a constant awareness of gratitude, not as an intellectual exercise, but as a lived experience. Each time you feel gratitude, you reinforce your connection to the intelligence that brings all things into being.

Holding the Vision

Your vision must be clear. Not vague, not uncertain, but distinct and definite. See it in your mind as already accomplished. Not as something distant, something that *might* happen, but as something real—something already yours.

This is not wishful thinking. It is not fantasy. It is the act of impressing the formless substance with a pattern of creation. You must live in the feeling of already having what you desire. You must let it fill your thoughts with certainty, just as the sun fills the sky with light.

In your quiet moments, return to this vision. Dwell in it. Feel it. And as you do, let gratitude arise naturally, for you will know that it is already taking shape in unseen ways.

Taking Aligned Action

You cannot simply think and expect things to materialize without action. However, action taken from a state of alignment differs from action taken from struggle. It is inspired, effortless, flowing.

Every day, do all that you can do but do not force. Do not act from fear or desperation—act from the quiet, knowing that what you desire is already moving toward you. Every action should be an expression of this knowing.

Whatever work you are engaged in now, do it fully. Bring presence to it. Make it excellent. Not because you are trying to impress others, not because you are seeking approval, but because in every moment, you are embodying the energy of increase.

Give more in use value than you receive in cash value. Infuse everything you do with life. Let your work, your interactions, and your presence itself communicate abundance.

The Law is Precise

This is not superstition. It is not blind faith. It is an exact process, just as reliable as the laws of physics. The results you receive will be in direct proportion to:

- The clarity of your vision – how distinctly you see what you want.
- The certainty of your purpose – how unwavering you are in your intent.
- The steadiness of your faith – how deeply you trust the process.
- The depth of your gratitude – how fully you align with the reality of abundance.

If you follow these principles, you will become rich. Not by chance. Not by luck. But because you are working in harmony with the fundamental nature of reality.

This is the Certain Way. It cannot fail.

Suggested Readings on Universal Laws and Manifestation

The following books offer a deep dive into the principles that govern abundance, success, and the nature of reality. These books expand upon the ideas presented in The Science of Getting Rich and provide further insights into how thought, energy, and belief shape our experiences.

Books on Universal Laws

The Kybalion – Three Initiates. A foundational text on Hermetic philosophy, this book explores the Seven Hermetic Principles, including Mentalism, Correspondence, Vibration, and Cause and Effect, which are essential to understanding the metaphysical laws that govern the universe.

Working with the Law – Raymond Holliwell Explores 11 universal laws, including the Law of Attraction, the Law of Supply, and the Law of Non-Resistance, providing practical steps to align with these forces for success and prosperity.

The Master Key System – Charles F. Haanel. A powerful guide that teaches how to harness the creative power of thought, based on universal laws. Many consider it one of the most influential books in the manifestation space.

The Secret Doctrine – Helena Blavatsky. A dense but profound work that explores esoteric knowledge, universal principles, and the deeper spiritual laws that shape reality.

The Game of Life and How to Play It – Florence Scovel Shinn. An easy-to-read yet profoundly effective book that explains how to use affirmation, faith, and universal laws to create a life of abundance.

Divine Magic: The Seven Sacred Secrets of Manifestation – Doreen Virtue. A modern interpretation of The Kybalion, offering practical ways to apply ancient wisdom to manifest success and well-being.

Books on Manifestation and Thought Power

The Power of Your Subconscious Mind – Joseph Murphy. One of the most widely read books on manifestation, this book explains how to reprogram your subconscious mind to attract wealth, success, and happiness.

The Magic of Believing – Claude M. Bristol. A powerful exploration of how belief and visualization shape reality, with compelling stories and examples.

Ask and It Is Given – Esther & Jerry Hicks. A fundamental book on the Law of Attraction, explaining how to align your vibration with what you desire through emotional awareness and intention.

It Works: The Famous Little Red Book That Makes Your Dreams Come True – R.H. Jarrett. A short but powerful book that lays out a simple three-step process for manifesting anything you want through focused thought.

You Are the Placebo – Dr. Joe Dispenza. A scientific take on manifestation, explaining how the mind and beliefs physically change reality at a quantum level.

Thought Vibration or The Law of Attraction in the Thought World – William Walker Atkinson. An early work on the Law of Attraction, explaining how focused thoughts and vibrations attract corresponding experiences.

Books on Energy, Frequency, and the Science of Manifestation

Reality Transurfing – Vadim Zeland. A deep and unconventional look at how reality works, explaining how to shift timelines and "surf" through reality by aligning with different energy states.

The Biology of Belief – Dr. Bruce Lipton. A groundbreaking book that explains how thoughts and beliefs influence biology, demonstrating the scientific foundation of manifestation.

E-Squared: Nine Do-It-Yourself Energy Experiments That Prove Your Thoughts Create Your Reality – Pam Grout A fun, interactive book that presents nine simple experiments to prove that thoughts shape reality.

Frequency: The Power of Personal Vibration – Penney Peirce. Explains how to raise your personal frequency to attract better experiences and align with your highest potential.

The Power of Awareness – Neville Goddard. A spiritual approach to manifestation, focusing on consciousness, imagination, and living as if your desires are already fulfilled.

Books on Spiritual Manifestation and Consciousness

A New Earth – Eckhart Tolle. Explores how presence, consciousness, and letting go of ego align you with a life of abundance and flow.

Becoming Supernatural – Dr. Joe Dispenza. Explains how to use meditation and neuroscience to tap into higher consciousness and manifest extraordinary experiences.

Creative Mind and Success – Ernest Holmes. A metaphysical guide that teaches how to align with divine intelligence and universal principles for personal and financial success.

Excuse Me, Your Life Is Waiting – Lynn Grabhorn. Focuses on the emotional aspect of manifestation, teaching how to maintain a high vibrational state to attract positive outcomes.

Metaphysical Bible Dictionary – Charles Fillmore. Explores biblical metaphysics and hidden meanings behind scriptural texts that relate to manifestation and universal laws.

Books on Quantum Physics and the Science of Reality Creation

The Field: The Quest for the Secret Force of the Universe – Lynne McTaggart. Explains how everything in the universe is connected through a quantum energy field and how this field responds to thoughts and intentions.

Quantum Success – Sandra Anne Taylor. Blends quantum physics with manifestation techniques, showing how energy and intention shape reality.

The Intention Experiment – Lynne McTaggart. A scientific exploration of how focused intention influences physical reality, based on real-world experiments.

What the Bleep Do We Know!? – William Arntz. A book that expands on the famous documentary, exploring consciousness, reality creation, and quantum manifestation.

The Holographic Universe – Michael Talbot. A mind-expanding book that suggests reality is holographic in nature and that consciousness plays a direct role in shaping the physical world.

Closing Thoughts

These books will deepen your understanding of the universal principles that govern wealth, success, and fulfillment. Whether you're looking for scientific, spiritual, or practical approaches to manifestation, this reading list will help you expand your awareness and refine your ability to consciously create the life you desire.

THE
SCIENCE OF
GETTING
RICH

W. D. WATTLES

FIRST PUBLISHED BY
ELIZABETH TOWNE
HOLYOKE, MASS.
1910

PREFACE.

This book is pragmatical, not philosophical; a practical manual, not a treatise upon theories. It is intended for the men and women whose most pressing need is for money; who wish to get rich first, and philosophize afterward. It is for those who have, so far, found neither the time, the means, nor the opportunity to go deeply into the study of metaphysics, but who want results and who are willing to take the conclusions of science as a basis for action, without going into all the processes by which those conclusions were reached.

It is expected that the reader will take the fundamental statements upon faith, just as he would take statements concerning a law of electrical action if they were promulgated by a Marconi or an Edison; and, taking the statements upon faith, that he will prove their truth by acting upon them without fear or hesitation. Every man or woman who does this will certainly get rich; for the science herein applied is an exact science, and failure is impossible. For the benefit, however, of those who wish to investigate philosophical theories and so secure a logical basis for faith, I will here cite certain authorities.

The monistic theory of the universe--the theory that One is All, and that All is One; that one Substance manifests itself as the seeming many elements of the material world--is of Hindu origin, and has been gradually winning its way into the thought of the western world for two hundred years. It is the foundation of all the Oriental philosophies, and of those of Descartes, Spinoza, Leibnitz, Schopenhauer, Hegel, and Emerson.

The reader who would dig to the philosophical foundations is advised to read Hegel and Emerson; and he will do well to read "The Eternal News," a very excellent pamphlet published by J. J. Brown, 300 Cathcart Road, Govanhill, Glasgow, Scotland. He may also find some help in a series of articles written by the author, which were published in *Nautilus* (Holyoke, Mass.) during the spring and summer of 1909, under the title "What is Truth?"

In writing this book I have sacrificed all other considerations to plainness and simplicity of style, so that all might understand. The plan of action laid down herein was deduced from the conclusions of philosophy; it has been thoroughly tested, and bears the supreme test of practical experiment; it works. If you wish to know how the conclusions were arrived at, read the writings of the authors mentioned above; and if you wish to reap the fruits of their philosophies in actual practice, read this book and do exactly as it tells you to do.

CHAPTER I.

THE RIGHT TO BE RICH.

Whatever may be said in praise of poverty, the fact remains that it is not possible to live a really complete or successful life unless one is rich. No man can rise to his greatest possible height in talent or soul development unless he has plenty of money; for to unfold the soul and to develop talent he must have many things to use, and he cannot have these things unless he has money to buy them with.

Man develops in mind, soul, and body by making use of things, and society is so organized that man must have money in order to become the possessor of things; therefore, the basis of all advancement for man must be the science of getting rich.

The object of all life is development; and everything that lives has an inalienable right to all the development it is capable of attaining.

Man's right to life means his right to have the free and unrestricted use of all the things which may be necessary to his fullest mental, spiritual, and physical unfoldment; or, in other words, his right to be rich.

In this book, I shall not speak of riches in a figurative way; to be really rich does not mean to be satisfied or contented with a little. No man ought to be satisfied with a little if he is capable of using and enjoying more. The purpose of Nature is the advancement and unfoldment of life; and every man should have all that can contribute to the power, elegance, beauty, and richness of life; to be content with less is sinful.

The man who owns all he wants for the living of all the life he is capable of living is rich; and no man who has not plenty of money can have all he wants. Life has advanced so far, and become so complex, that even the most ordinary man or woman requires a great amount of wealth in order to live in a manner that even approaches completeness. Every person naturally wants to become all that he is capable of becoming; this desire to realize innate possibilities is inherent in human nature; we cannot help wanting to be all that we can be. Success in life is becoming what you want to be; you can become what you want to be only by making use of things, and you can have the free use of things only as you become rich enough to buy them. To understand the science of getting rich is therefore the most essential of all knowledge.

There is nothing wrong in wanting to get rich. The desire for riches is really the desire for a richer, fuller, and more abundant life; and that desire is praiseworthy. The man who does not desire to live more abundantly is abnormal, and so the man who does not desire to have money enough to buy all he wants is abnormal.

There are three motives for which we live; we live for the body, we live for the mind, and we live for the soul. No one of these is better or holier than the other; all are alike desirable, and no one of the three--body, mind, or soul--can live fully if either of the others is cut short of full life and expression. It is not right or noble to live only for the soul and deny mind or body; and it is wrong to live for the intellect and deny body and soul.

We are all acquainted with the loathsome consequences of living for the body and denying both mind and soul; and we see that real life means the complete expression of all that man can give forth through body, mind, and soul. Whatever he may say, no man can be really happy or satisfied unless his body is living fully in every function, and unless the same is true of his mind and his soul. Wherever there is unexpressed possibility, or function not performed, there is unsatisfied desire. Desire is possibility seeking expression, or function seeking performance.

Man cannot live fully in body without good food, comfortable clothing, and warm shelter; and without freedom from excessive toil. Rest and recreation are also necessary to his physical life.

He cannot live fully in mind without books and time to study them, without opportunity for travel and observation, or without intellectual companionship.

To live fully in mind he must have intellectual recreations, and must surround himself with all the objects of art and beauty he is capable of using and appreciating.

To live fully in soul, man must have love; and love is denied expression by poverty.

Man's highest happiness is found in the bestowal of benefits on those he loves; love finds its most natural and spontaneous expression in giving. The man who has nothing to give cannot fill his place as a husband or father, as a citizen, or as a man. It is in the use of material things that man finds full life for his body, develops his mind, and unfolds his soul. It is therefore of supreme importance to him that he should be rich.

It is perfectly right that you should desire to be rich; if you are a normal man or woman you cannot help doing so. It is perfectly right that you should give your best attention to the Science of Getting Rich, for it is the noblest and most necessary of all studies. If you neglect this study, you are derelict in your duty to yourself, to God, and to humanity; for you can render God and humanity no greater service than to make the most of yourself.

CHAPTER II.

THERE IS A SCIENCE OF GETTING RICH.

There is a Science of getting rich, and it is an exact science, like algebra or arithmetic. There are certain laws which govern the process of acquiring riches; once these laws are learned and obeyed by any man, he will get rich with mathematical certainty.

The ownership of money and property comes as a result of doing things in a certain way; those who do things in this Certain Way, whether on purpose or accidentally, get rich; while those who do not do things in this Certain Way, no matter how hard they work or how able they are, remain poor.

It is a natural law that like causes always produce like effects; and, therefore, any man or woman who learns to do things in this Certain Way will infallibly get rich.

That the above statement is true is shown by the following facts:

Getting rich is not a matter of environment, for, if it were, all the people in certain neighborhoods would become wealthy; the people of one city would all be rich, while those of other towns would all be poor; or the inhabitants of one state would roll in wealth, while those of an adjoining state would be in poverty.

But everywhere we see rich and poor living side by side, in the same environment, and often engaged in the same vocations. When two men are in the same locality, and in the same business, and one gets rich while the other remains poor, it shows that getting rich is not, primarily, a matter of environment. Some environments may be more favorable than others, but when two men in the same business are in the same neighborhood, and one gets rich while the other fails, it indicates that getting rich is the result of doing things in a Certain Way.

And further, the ability to do things in this Certain Way is not due solely to the possession of talent, for many people who have great talent remain poor, while others who have very little talent get rich.

Studying the people who have got rich, we find that they are an average lot in all respects, having no greater talents and abilities than other men. It is evident that they do not get rich because they possess talents and abilities that other men have not, but because they happen to do things in a Certain Way.

Getting rich is not the result of saving, or "thrift"; many very penurious people are poor, while free spenders often get rich.

Nor is getting rich due to doing things which others fail to do; for two men in the same business often do almost exactly the same things, and one gets rich while the other remains poor or becomes a bankrupt.

From all these things, we must come to the conclusion that getting rich is the result of doing things in a Certain Way.

If getting rich is the result of doing things in a Certain Way, and if like causes always produce like effects, then any man or woman who can do things in that way can become rich, and the whole matter is brought within the domain of exact science.

The question arises here, whether this Certain Way may not be so difficult that only a few may follow it. This cannot be true, as we have seen, so far as natural ability is concerned. Talented people get rich, and blockheads get rich; intellectually brilliant people get rich, and very stupid people get rich; physically strong people get rich, and weak and sickly people get rich.

Some degree of ability to think and understand is, of course, essential; but in so far as natural ability is concerned, any man or woman who has sense enough to read and understand these words can certainly get rich.

Also, we have seen that it is not a matter of environment. Location counts for something; one would not go to the heart of the Sahara and expect to do successful business.

Getting rich involves the necessity of dealing with men, and of being where there are people to deal with; and if these people are inclined to deal in the way you want to deal, so much the better. But that is about as far as environment goes.

If anybody else in your town can get rich, so can you; and if anybody else in your state can get rich, so can you.

Again, it is not a matter of choosing some particular business or profession. People get rich in every business and in every profession, while their next-door neighbors in the same vocation remain in poverty.

It is true that you will do best in a business which you like, and which is congenial to you; and if you have certain talents which are well developed, you will do best in a business which calls for the exercise of those talents.

Also, you will do best in a business which is suited to your locality; an ice-cream parlor would do better in a warm climate than in Greenland, and a salmon fishery will succeed better in the Northwest than in Florida, where there are no salmon.

But, aside from these general limitations, getting rich is not dependent upon your engaging in some particular business, but upon your learning to do things in a Certain Way. If you are now in business, and anybody else in your locality is getting rich in the same business, while you are *not* getting rich, it is because you are not doing things in the same Way that the other person is doing them.

No one is prevented from getting rich by lack of capital. True, as you get capital the increase becomes more easy and rapid; but one who has capital is already rich, and does not need to consider how to become so. No matter how poor you may be, if you begin to do things in the Certain Way you will begin to get rich; and you will begin to have capital. The getting of capital is a part of the process of getting rich; and it is a part of the result which invariably follows the doing of things in the Certain Way.

You may be the poorest man on the continent, and be deeply in debt; you may have neither friends, influence, nor resources; but if you begin to do things in this Way, you must infallibly begin to get rich, for like causes must produce like effects. If you have no capital, you can get capital; if you are in the wrong business, you can get into the right business; if you are in the wrong location, you can go to the right location; and you can do so *by beginning in your present business and in your present location* to do things in the Certain Way which causes success.

CHAPTER III.

IS OPPORTUNITY MONOPOLIZED?

No man is kept poor because opportunity has been taken away from him; because other people have monopolized the wealth, and have put a fence around it. You may be shut off from engaging in business in certain lines, but there are other channels open to you. Probably it would be hard for you to get control of any of the great railroad systems; that field is pretty well monopolized. But the electric railway business is still in its infancy, and offers plenty of scope for enterprise; and it will be but a very few years until traffic and transportation through the air will become a great industry, and in all its branches will give employment to hundreds of thousands, and perhaps to millions, of people. Why not turn your attention to the development of aerial transportation, instead of competing with J. J. Hill and others for a chance in the steam railway world?

It is quite true that if you are a workman in the employ of the steel trust you have very little chance of becoming the owner of the plant in which you work; but it is also true that if you will commence to act in a Certain Way, you can soon leave the employ of the steel trust; you can buy a farm of from ten to forty acres, and engage in business as a producer of foodstuffs. There is great opportunity at this time for men who will live upon small tracts of land and cultivate the same intensively; such men will certainly get rich. You may say that it is impossible for you to get the land, but I am going to prove to you that it is not impossible, and that you can certainly get a farm if you will go to work in a Certain Way.

At different periods the tide of opportunity sets in different directions, according to the needs of the Whole, and the particular stage of social evolution which has been reached. At present, in America, it is setting toward agriculture and the allied industries and professions. To-day, opportunity is open before the farmer in his line more than before the factory worker in his line. It is open before the business man who supplies the farmer more than before the one who supplies the factory worker; and before the professional man who waits upon the farmer more than before the one who serves the working class.

There is abundance of opportunity for the man who will go with the tide, instead of trying to swim against it.

So the factory workers, either as individuals or as a class, are not deprived of opportunity. The workers are not being "kept down" by their masters; they are not being "ground" by the trusts and combinations of capital. As a class, they are where they are because they do not do things in a Certain Way. If the workers of America chose to do so, they could follow the example of their brothers in Belgium and other countries, and establish great department stores and co-operative industries; they could elect men of their own class to office, and pass laws favoring the development of such co-operative industries; and in a few years they could take peaceable possession of the industrial field.

The working class may become the master class whenever they will begin to do things in a Certain Way; the law of wealth is the same for them as it is for all others. This they must learn; and they will remain where they are as long as they continue to do as they do. The individual worker, however, is not held down by the ignorance or the mental slothfulness of his class; he can follow the tide of opportunity to riches, and this book will tell him how.

No one is kept in poverty by a shortness in the supply of riches; there is more than enough for all. A palace as large as the capitol at Washington might be built for every family on earth from the building material in the United States alone; and under intensive cultivation, this country would produce wool, cotton, linen, and silk enough to clothe each person in the world finer than Solomon was arrayed in all his glory;

together with food enough to feed them all luxuriously. The visible supply is practically inexhaustible; and the invisible supply really IS inexhaustible.

Everything you see on earth is made from one original substance, out of which all things proceed.

New forms are constantly being made, and older ones are dissolving; but all are shapes assumed by One Thing.

There is no limit to the supply of Formless Stuff, or Original Substance. The universe is made out of it; but it was not all used in making the universe. The spaces in, through, and between the forms of the visible universe are permeated and filled with the Original

Substance; with the Formless Stuff; with the raw material of all things. Ten thousand times as much as has been made might still be made, and even then we should not have exhausted the supply of universal raw material.

No man, therefore, is poor because nature is poor, or because there is not enough to go around.

Nature is an inexhaustible storehouse of riches; the supply will never run short. Original Substance is alive with creative energy, and is constantly producing more forms. When the supply of building material is exhausted, more will be produced; when the soil is exhausted so that foodstuffs and materials for clothing will no longer grow upon it, it will be renewed or more soil will be made. When all the gold and silver has been dug from the earth, if man is still in such a stage of social development that he needs gold and silver, more will be produced from the Formless. The Formless Stuff responds to the needs of man; it will not let him be without any good thing.

This is true of man collectively; the race as a whole is always abundantly rich, and if individuals are poor, it is because they do not follow the Certain Way of doing things which makes the individual man rich.

The Formless Stuff is intelligent; it is stuff which thinks. It is alive, and is always impelled toward more life.

It is the natural and inherent impulse of life to seek to live more; it is the nature of intelligence to enlarge itself, and of consciousness to seek to extend its boundaries and find fuller expression. The universe of forms has been made by Formless Living Substance, throwing itself into form in order to express itself more fully.

The universe is a great Living Presence, always moving inherently toward more life and fuller functioning.

Nature is formed for the advancement of life; its impelling motive is the increase of life. For this cause, everything which can possibly minister to life is bountifully provided; there can be no lack unless God is to contradict himself and nullify his own works.

You are not kept poor by lack in the supply of riches; it is a fact which I shall demonstrate a little farther on that even the resources of the Formless Supply are at the command of the man or woman who will act and think in a Certain Way.

CHAPTER IV.

THE FIRST PRINCIPLE IN THE SCIENCE OF GETTING RICH.

Thought is the only power which can produce tangible riches from the Formless Substance. The stuff from which all things are made is a substance which thinks, and a thought of form in this substance produces the form.

Original Substance moves according to its thoughts; every form and process you see in nature is the visible expression of a thought in Original Substance. As the Formless Stuff thinks of a form, it takes that form; as it thinks of a motion, it makes that motion. That is the way all things were created. We live in a thought world, which is part of a thought universe.

The thought of a moving universe extended throughout Formless Substance, and the Thinking Stuff moving according to that thought, took the form of systems of planets, and maintains that form. Thinking Substance takes the form of its thought, and moves according to the thought. Holding the idea of a circling system of suns and worlds, it takes the form of these bodies, and moves them as it thinks. Thinking the form of a slow-growing oak tree, it moves accordingly, and produces the tree, though centuries may be required to do the work. In creating, the Formless seems to move according to the lines of motion it has established; the thought of an oak tree does not cause the instant formation of a full-grown tree, but it does start in motion the forces which will produce the tree, along established lines of growth.

Every thought of form, held in thinking Substance, causes the creation of the form, but always, or at least generally, along lines of growth and action already established.

The thought of a house of a certain construction, if it were impressed upon Formless Substance, might not cause the instant formation of the house; but it would cause the turning of creative energies already working in trade and commerce into such channels as to result in the speedy building of the house. And if there were no existing channels through which the creative energy could work, then the house would be formed directly from primal substance, without waiting for the slow processes of the organic and inorganic world.

No thought of form can be impressed upon Original Substance without causing the creation of the form.

Man is a thinking center, and can originate thought. All the forms that man fashions with his hands must first exist in his thought; he cannot shape a thing until he has thought that thing.

And so far man has confined his efforts wholly to the work of his hands; he has applied manual labor to the world of forms, seeking to change or modify those already existing. He has never thought of trying to cause the creation of new forms by impressing his thoughts upon Formless Substance.

When man has a thought-form, he takes material from the forms of nature, and makes an image of the form which is in his mind. He has, so far, made little or no effort to co-operate with Formless Intelligence; to work "with the Father." He has not dreamed that he can "do what he seeth the Father doing." Man re-shapes and modifies existing forms by manual labor; he has given no attention to the question whether he may not produce things from Formless Substance by communicating his thoughts to it. We propose to prove that he may do so; to prove that any man or woman may do so, and to show how. As our first step, we must lay down three fundamental propositions.

First, we assert that there is one original formless stuff, or substance, from which all things are made. All the seemingly many elements are but different presentations of one element; all the many forms found in organic and inorganic nature are but different shapes, made from the same stuff. And this stuff is thinking stuff; a thought held in it produces the form of the thought. Thought, in thinking substance, produces shapes. Man is a thinking center, capable of original thought; if man can communicate his thought to original thinking substance, he can cause the creation, or formation, of the thing he thinks about. To summarize this:

There is a thinking stuff from which all things are made, and which, in its original state, permeates, penetrates, and fills the interspaces of the universe.

A thought, in this substance, produces the thing that is imaged by the thought.

Man can form things in his thought, and, by impressing his thought upon formless substance, can cause the thing he thinks about to be created.

It may be asked if I can prove these statements; and without going into details, I answer that I can do so, both by logic and experience.

Reasoning back from the phenomena of form and thought, I come to one original thinking substance; and reasoning forward from this thinking substance, I come to man's power to cause the formation of the thing he thinks about.

And by experiment, I find the reasoning true; and this is my strongest proof.

If one man who reads this book gets rich by doing what it tells him to do, that is evidence in support of my claim; but if every man who does what it tells him to do gets rich, that is positive proof until some one goes through the process and fails. The theory is true until the process fails; and this process will not fail, for every man who does exactly what this book tells him to do will get rich.

I have said that men get rich by doing things in a Certain Way; and in order to do so, men must become able to think in a certain way.

A man's way of doing things is the direct result of the way he thinks about things.

To do things in the way you want to do them, you will have to acquire the ability to think the way you want to think; this is the first step toward getting rich.

To think what you want to think is to think TRUTH, regardless of appearances.

Every man has the natural and inherent power to think what he wants to think, but it requires far more effort to do so than it does to think the thoughts which are suggested by appearances. To think according to appearances is easy; to think truth regardless of appearances is laborious, and requires the expenditure of more power than any other work man is called upon to perform.

There is no labor from which most people shrink as they do from that of sustained and consecutive thought; it is the hardest work in the world. This is especially true when truth is contrary to appearances. Every appearance in the visible world tends to produce a corresponding form in the mind which observes it; and this can only be prevented by holding the thought of the TRUTH.

To look upon the appearance of disease will produce the form of disease in your own mind, and ultimately in your body, unless you hold the thought of the truth, which is that there is no disease; it is only an appearance, and the reality is health.

To look upon the appearances of poverty will produce corresponding forms in your own mind, unless you hold to the truth that there is no poverty; there is only abundance.

To think health when surrounded by the appearances of disease, or to think riches when in the midst of appearances of poverty, requires power; but he who acquires this power becomes a MASTER MIND. He can conquer fate; he can have what he wants.

This power can only be acquired by getting hold of the basic fact which is behind all appearances; and that fact is that there is one Thinking Substance, from which and by which all things are made.

Then we must grasp the truth that every thought held in this substance becomes a form, and that man can so impress his thoughts upon It as to cause them to take form and become visible things.

When we realize this, we lose all doubt and fear, for we know that we can create what we want to create; we can get what we want to have, and can become what we want to be. As a first step toward getting rich, you must believe the three fundamental statements given previously in this chapter; and in order to emphasize them, I repeat them here:

There is a thinking stuff from which all things are made, and which, in its original state, permeates, penetrates, and fills the interspaces of the universe.

A thought, in this substance, produces the thing that is imaged by the thought.

Man can form things in his thought, and, by impressing his thought upon formless substance, can cause the thing he thinks about to be created.

You must lay aside all other concepts of the universe than this monistic one; and you must dwell upon this until it is fixed in your mind, and has become your habitual thought. Read these creed statements over and over again; fix every word upon your memory, and meditate upon them until you firmly believe what they say. If a doubt comes to you, cast it aside as a sin. Do not listen to arguments against this idea; do not go to churches or lectures where a contrary concept of things is taught or preached. Do not read magazines or books which teach a different idea; if you get mixed up in your faith, all your efforts will be in vain.

Do not ask why these things are true, nor speculate as to how they can be true; simply take them on trust.

The science of getting rich begins with the absolute acceptance of this faith.

CHAPTER V.

INCREASING LIFE.

You must get rid of the last vestige of the old idea that there is a Deity whose will it is that you should be poor, or whose purposes may be served by keeping you in poverty.

The Intelligent Substance which is All, and in all, and which lives in All and lives in you, is a consciously Living Substance. Being a consciously living substance, It must have the natural and inherent desire of every living intelligence for increase of life. Every living thing must continually seek for the enlargement of its life, because life, in the mere act of living, must increase itself.

A seed, dropped into the ground, springs into activity, and in the act of living produces a hundred more seeds; life, by living, multiplies itself. It is forever Becoming More; it must do so, if it continues to be at all.

Intelligence is under this same necessity for continuous increase. Every thought we think makes it necessary for us to think another thought; consciousness is continually expanding. Every fact we learn leads us to the learning of another fact; knowledge is continually increasing. Every talent we cultivate brings to the mind the desire to cultivate another talent; we are subject to the urge of life, seeking expression, which ever drives us on to know more, to do more, and to be more.

In order to know more, do more, and be more we must have more; we must have things to use, for we learn, and do, and become, only by using things. We must get rich, so that we can live more.

The desire for riches is simply the capacity for larger life seeking fulfillment; every desire is the effort of an unexpressed possibility to come into action. It is power seeking to manifest which causes desire. That which makes you want more money is the same as that which makes the plant grow; it is Life, seeking fuller expression.

The One Living Substance must be subject to this inherent law of all life; it is permeated with the desire to live more; that is why it is under the necessity of creating things.

The One Substance desires to live more in you; hence it wants you to have all the things you can use.

It is the desire of God that you should get rich. He wants you to get rich because he can express himself better through you if you have plenty of things to use in giving him expression. He can live more in you if you have unlimited command of the means of life.

The universe desires you to have everything you want to have.

Nature is friendly to your plans.

Everything is naturally for you.

Make up your mind that this is true.

It is essential, however, that *your purpose should harmonize with the purpose that is in All.*

You must want real life, not mere pleasure or sensual gratification. Life is the performance of function; and the individual really lives only when he performs every function, physical, mental, and spiritual, of which he is capable, without excess in any.

You do not want to get rich in order to live swinishly, for the gratification of animal desires; that is not life. But the performance of every physical function is a part of life, and no one lives completely who denies the impulses of the body a normal and healthful expression.

You do not want to get rich solely to enjoy mental pleasures, to get knowledge, to gratify ambition, to outshine others, to be famous. All these are a legitimate part of life, but the man who lives for the pleasures of the intellect alone will only have a partial life, and he will never be satisfied with his lot.

You do not want to get rich solely for the good of others, to lose yourself for the salvation of mankind, to experience the joys of philanthropy and sacrifice. The joys of the soul are only a part of life; and they are no better or nobler than any other part.

You want to get rich in order that you may eat, drink, and be merry when it is time to do these things; in order that you may surround yourself with beautiful things, see distant lands, feed your mind, and develop your intellect; in order that you may love men and do kind things, and be able to play a good part in helping the world to find truth.

But remember that extreme altruism is no better and no nobler than extreme selfishness; both are mistakes.

Get rid of the idea that God wants you to sacrifice yourself for others, and that you can secure his favor by doing so; God requires nothing of the kind.

What he wants is that you should make the most of yourself, for yourself, and for others; and *you can help others more by making the most of yourself than in any other way.*

You can make the most of yourself only by getting rich; so it is right and praiseworthy that you should give your first and best thought to the work of acquiring wealth.

Remember, however, that the desire of Substance is for all, and its movements must be for more life to all; it cannot be made to work for less life to any, because it is equally in all, seeking riches and life.

Intelligent Substance will make things for you, but it will not take things away from some one else and give them to you.

You must get rid of the thought of competition. You are to create, not to compete for what is already created.

You do not have to take anything away from any one.

You do not have to drive sharp bargains.

You do not have to cheat, or to take advantage. You do not need to let any man work for you for less than he earns.

You do not have to covet the property of others, or to look at it with wishful eyes; no man has anything of which you cannot have the like, and that without taking what he has away from him.

You are to become a creator, not a competitor; you are going to get what you want, but in such a way that when you get it every other man will have more than he has now.

I am aware that there are men who get a vast amount of money by proceeding in direct opposition to the statements in the paragraph above, and may add a word of explanation here. Men of the plutocratic type, who become very rich, do so sometimes purely by their extraordinary ability on the plane of competition; and sometimes they unconsciously relate themselves to Substance in its great purposes and movements for the general racial upbuilding through industrial evolution. Rockefeller, Carnegie, Morgan, *et al.*, have been the unconscious agents of the Supreme in the necessary work of systematizing and organizing productive industry; and in the end, their work will contribute immensely toward increased life for all. Their day is nearly over; they have organized production, and *will soon be succeeded by the agents of the multitude, who will organize the machinery of distribution.*

The multi-millionaires are like the monster reptiles of the prehistoric eras; they play a necessary part in the evolutionary process, but the same Power which produced them will dispose of them. And it is well to bear in mind that they have never been really rich; a record of the private lives of most of this class will show that they have really been the most abject and wretched of the poor.

Riches secured on the competitive plane are never satisfactory and permanent; they are yours to-day, and another's to-morrow. Remember, if you are to become rich in a scientific and certain way, you must rise entirely out of the competitive thought. You must never think for a moment that the supply is limited. Just as soon as you begin to think that all the money is being "cornered" and controlled by bankers and others, and that you must exert yourself to get laws passed to stop this process, and so on; in that moment you drop into the competitive mind, and your power to cause creation is gone for the time being; and what is worse, you will probably arrest the creative movements you have already instituted.

KNOW that there are countless millions of dollars' worth of gold in the mountains of the earth, not yet brought to light; and know that if there were not, more would be created from Thinking Substance to supply your needs.

KNOW that the money you need will come, even if it is necessary for a thousand men to be led to the discovery of new gold mines to-morrow.

Never look at the visible supply; look always at the limitless riches in Formless Substance, and KNOW that they are coming to you as fast as you can receive and use them. Nobody, by cornering the visible supply, can prevent you from getting what is yours.

So never allow yourself to think for an instant that all the best building spots will be taken before you get ready to build your house, unless you hurry. Never worry about the trusts and combines, and get anxious for fear they will soon come to own the whole earth. Never get afraid that you will lose what you want because some other person "beats you to it." That cannot possibly happen; you are not seeking anything that is possessed by anybody else; you are causing what you want to be created from Formless Substance, and the supply is without limits. Stick to the formulated statement:

There is a thinking stuff from which all things are made, and which, in its original state, permeates, penetrates, and fills the interspaces of the universe.

A thought, in this substance, produces the thing that is imaged by the thought.

Man can form things in his thought, and, by impressing his thought upon formless substance, can cause the thing he thinks about to be created.

CHAPTER VI.

HOW RICHES COME TO YOU.

When I say that you do not have to drive sharp bargains, I do not mean that you do not have to drive any bargains at all, or that you are above the necessity for having any dealings with your fellow men. I mean that you will not need to deal with them unfairly; you do not have to get something for nothing, *but can give to every man more than you take from him.*

You cannot give every man more in cash market value than you take from him, but you can give him more in use value than the cash value of the thing you take from him. The paper, ink, and other material in this book may not be worth the money you paid for it; but if the ideas suggested by it bring you thousands of dollars, you have not been wronged by those who sold it to you; they have given you a great use value for a small cash value.

Let us suppose that I own a picture by one of the great artists, which, in any civilized community, is worth thousands of dollars. I take it to Baffin Bay, and by "salesmanship" induce an Eskimo to give a bundle of furs worth $500 for it. I have really wronged him, for he has no use for the picture; it has no use value to him; it will not add to his life.

But suppose I give him a gun worth $50 for his furs; then he has made a good bargain. He has use for the gun; it will get him many more furs and much food; it will add to his life in every way; it will make him rich.

When you rise from the competitive to the creative plane, you can scan your business transactions very strictly, and if you are selling any man anything which does not add more to his life than the thing he gives you in exchange, you can afford to stop it. You do not have to beat anybody in business. And if you are in a business which does beat people, get out of it at once.

Give every man more in use value than you take from him in cash value; then you are adding to the life of the world by every business transaction.

If you have people working for you, you must take from them more in cash value than you pay them in wages; but *you can so organize your business that it will be filled with the principle of advancement*, and so that each employee who wishes to do so may advance a little every day.

You can make your business do for your employees what this book is doing for you. You can so conduct your business that it will be a sort of ladder, by which every employee who will take the trouble may climb to riches himself; and given the opportunity, if he will not do so it is not your fault.

And finally, because you are to cause the creation of your riches from Formless Substance which permeates all your environment, it does not follow that they are to take shape from the atmosphere and come into being before your eyes.

If you want a sewing machine, for instance, I do not mean to tell you that you are to impress the thought of a sewing machine on Thinking Substance until the machine is formed without hands, in the room where you sit, or elsewhere. But if you want a sewing machine, hold the mental image of it with the most positive certainty that it is being made, or is on its way to you. After once forming the thought, have the most absolute and unquestioning faith that the sewing machine is coming; never think of it, or speak of it, in any other way than as being sure to arrive. Claim it as already yours.

It will be brought to you by the power of the Supreme Intelligence, acting upon the minds of men. If you live in Maine, it may be that a man will be brought from Texas or Japan to engage in some transaction which will result in your getting what you want.

If so, the whole matter will be as much to that man's advantage as it is to yours.

Do not forget for a moment that the Thinking Substance is through all, in all, communicating with all, and can influence all. The desire of Thinking Substance for fuller life and better living has caused the creation of all the sewing machines already made; and it can cause the creation of millions more, and will, whenever men set it in motion by desire and faith, and by acting in a Certain Way.

You can certainly have a sewing machine in your house; and it is just as certain that you can have any other thing or things which you want, and which you will use for the advancement of your own life and the lives of others.

You need not hesitate about asking largely; "it is your Father's pleasure to give you the kingdom," said Jesus.

Original Substance wants to live all that is possible in you, and wants you to have all that you can or will use for the living of the most abundant life.

If you fix upon your consciousness the fact that the desire you feel for the possession of riches is one with the desire of Omnipotence for more complete expression, your faith becomes invincible.

Once I saw a little boy sitting at a piano, and vainly trying to bring harmony out of the keys; and I saw that he was grieved and provoked by his inability to play real music. I asked him the cause of his vexation, and he answered, "I can feel the music in me, but I can't make my hands go right." The music in him was the URGE of Original Substance, containing all the possibilities of all life; all that there is of music was seeking expression through the child.

God, the One Substance, is trying to live and do and enjoy things through humanity. He is saying, "I want hands to build wonderful structures, to play divine harmonies, to paint glorious pictures; I want feet to run my errands, eyes to see my beauties, tongues to tell mighty truths and to sing marvelous songs," and so on.

All that there is of possibility is seeking expression through men. God wants those who can play music to have pianos and every other instrument, and to have the means to cultivate their talents to the fullest extent; He wants those who can appreciate beauty to be able to surround themselves with beautiful things; He wants those who can discern truth to have every opportunity to travel and observe; He wants those who can appreciate dress to be beautifully clothed, and those who can appreciate good food to be luxuriously fed.

He wants all these things because it is Himself that enjoys and appreciates them; it is God who wants to play, and sing, and enjoy beauty, and proclaim truth, and wear fine clothes, and eat good foods.

"It is God that worketh in you to will and to do," said Paul. The desire you feel for riches is the Infinite, seeking to express Himself in you as He sought to find expression in the little boy at the piano.

So you need not hesitate to ask largely.

Your part is to focalize and express the desires of God.

This is a difficult point with most people; they retain something of the old idea that poverty and self-sacrifice are pleasing to God. They look upon poverty as a part of the plan, a necessity of nature. They have the idea that God has finished His work, and made all that He can make, and that the majority of men must stay poor because there is not enough to go around. They hold to so much of this erroneous thought that they feel ashamed to ask for wealth; they try not to want more than a very modest competence, just enough to make them fairly comfortable.

I recall now the case of one student who was told that he must get in mind a clear picture of the things he desired, so that the creative thought of them might be impressed on Formless Substance. He was a very poor man, living in a rented house, and having only what he earned from day to day; and he could not grasp the fact that all wealth was his. So, after thinking the matter over, he decided that he might reasonably ask for a new rug for the floor of his best room, and an anthracite coal stove to heat the house during the cold weather. Following the instructions given in this book, he obtained these things in a few months; and then it dawned upon him that he had not asked enough. He went through the house in which he lived, and planned all the improvements he would like to make in it; he mentally added a bay window here and a room there, until it was complete in his mind as his ideal home; and then he planned its furnishings.

Holding the whole picture in his mind, he began living in the Certain Way, and moving toward what he wanted; and he owns the house now, and is rebuilding it after the form of his mental image. And now, with still larger faith, he is going on to get greater things. It has been unto him according to his faith, and it is so with you and with all of us.

CHAPTER VII.

GRATITUDE.

The illustrations given in the last chapter will have conveyed to the reader the fact that the first step toward getting rich is to convey the idea of your wants to the Formless Substance.

This is true, and you will see that in order to do so it becomes necessary to relate yourself to the Formless Intelligence in a harmonious way.

To secure this harmonious relation is a matter of such primary and vital importance that I shall give some space to its discussion here, and give you instructions which, if you will follow them, will be certain to bring you into perfect unity of mind with God.

The whole process of mental adjustment and atonement can be summed up in one word, *gratitude*.

First, you believe that there is one Intelligent Substance, from which all things proceed; second, you believe that this

Substance gives you everything you desire; and third, you relate yourself to It by a feeling of deep and profound gratitude.

Many people who order their lives rightly in all other ways are kept in poverty by their lack of gratitude. Having received one gift from God, they cut the wires which connect them with Him by failing to make acknowledgment.

It is easy to understand that the nearer we live to the source of wealth, the more wealth we shall receive; and it is easy also to understand that the soul that is always grateful lives in closer touch with God than the one which never looks to Him in thankful acknowledgment.

The more gratefully we fix our minds on the Supreme when good things come to us, the more good things we will receive, and the more rapidly they will come; and the reason simply is that the mental attitude of gratitude draws the mind into closer touch with the source from which the blessings come.

If it is a new thought to you that gratitude brings your whole mind into closer harmony with the creative energies of the universe, consider it well, and you will see that it is true. The good things you already have have come to you along the line of obedience to certain laws. Gratitude will lead your mind out along the ways by which things come; and it will keep you in close harmony with creative thought and prevent you from falling into competitive thought.

Gratitude alone can keep you looking toward the All, and prevent you from falling into the error of thinking of the supply as limited; and to do that would be fatal to your hopes.

There is a Law of Gratitude, and it is absolutely necessary that you should observe the law, if you are to get the results you seek.

The law of gratitude is the natural principle that action and reaction are always equal, and in opposite directions.

The grateful outreaching of your mind in thankful praise to the Supreme *is a liberation or expenditure of force; it cannot fail to reach that to which it is addressed, and the reaction is an instantaneous movement toward you.*

"Draw nigh unto God, and He will draw nigh unto you." That is a statement of psychological truth.

And if your gratitude is strong and constant, the reaction in Formless Substance will be strong and continuous; the movement of the things you want will be always toward you. Notice the grateful attitude that Jesus took; how He always seems to be saying, "I thank Thee, Father, that Thou hearest me." You cannot exercise much power without gratitude; for it is gratitude that keeps you connected with Power.

But the value of gratitude does not consist solely in getting you more blessings in the future. Without gratitude you cannot long keep from dissatisfied thought regarding things as they are.

The moment you permit your mind to dwell with dissatisfaction upon things as they are, you begin to lose ground. You fix attention upon the common, the ordinary, the poor, and the squalid and mean; and your mind takes the form of these things. Then you will transmit these forms or mental images to the Formless, and the common, the poor, the squalid, and mean will come to you.

To permit your mind to dwell upon the inferior is to become inferior and to surround yourself with inferior things.

On the other hand, to fix your attention on the best is to surround yourself with the best, and to become the best.

The Creative Power within us makes us into the image of that to which we give our attention.

We are Thinking Substance, and thinking substance always takes the form of that which it thinks about.

The grateful mind is constantly fixed upon the best; therefore it tends to become the best; it takes the form or character of the best, and will receive the best.

Also, faith is born of gratitude. The grateful mind continually expects good things, and expectation becomes faith. The reaction of gratitude upon one's own mind produces faith; and every outgoing wave of grateful thanksgiving increases faith. He who has no feeling of gratitude cannot long retain a living faith; and without a living faith you cannot get rich by the creative method, as we shall see in the following chapters.

It is necessary, then, to cultivate the habit of being grateful for every good thing that comes to you; and to give thanks continuously.

And because all things have contributed to your advancement, you should include all things in your gratitude.

Do not waste time thinking or talking about the shortcomings or wrong actions of plutocrats or trust magnates. Their organization of the world has made your opportunity; all you get really comes to you because of them.

Do not rage against corrupt politicians; if it were not for politicians we should fall into anarchy, and your opportunity would be greatly lessened.

God has worked a long time and very patiently to bring us up to where we are in industry and government, and He is going right on with His work. There is not the least doubt that

He will do away with plutocrats, trust magnates, captains of industry, and politicians as soon as they can be spared; but in the meantime, behold they are all very good. Remember that they are all helping to arrange the lines of transmission along which your riches will come to you, and be grateful to them all. This will bring you into harmonious relations with the good in everything, and the good in everything will move toward you.

CHAPTER VIII.

THINKING IN THE CERTAIN WAY.

Turn back to chapter VI., and read again the story of the man who formed a mental image of his house, and you will get a fair idea of the initial step toward getting rich. You must form a clear and definite mental picture of what you want; you cannot transmit an idea unless you have it yourself. You must have it before you can give it; and many people fail to impress Thinking Substance because they have themselves only a vague and misty concept of the things they want to do, to have, or to become.

It is not enough that you should have a general desire for wealth "to do good with"; everybody has that desire.

It is not enough that you should have a wish to travel, see things, live more, etc. Everybody has those desires also. If you were going to send a wireless message to a friend, you would not send the letters of the alphabet in their order, and let him construct the message for himself; nor would you take words at random from the dictionary. You would send a coherent sentence; one which meant something. When you try to impress your wants upon Substance, remember that it must be done by a coherent statement; you must know what you want, and be definite.

You can never get rich, or start the creative power into action, by sending out unformed longings and vague desires.

Go over your desires just as the man I have described went over his house; see just what you want, and get a clear mental picture of it as you wish it to look when you get it.

That clear mental picture you must have continually in mind, as the sailor has in mind the port toward which he is sailing the ship; you must keep your face toward it all the time. You must no more lose sight of it than the steersman loses sight of the compass.

It is not necessary to take exercises in concentration, nor to set apart special times for prayer and affirmation, nor to "go into the silence," nor to do occult stunts of any kind. These things are well enough, but all you need is to know what you want, and to want it badly enough so that it will stay in your thoughts.

Spend as much of your leisure time as you can in contemplating your picture, but no one needs to take exercises to concentrate his mind on a thing which he really wants; it is the things you do not really care about which require effort to fix your attention upon them.

And unless you really want to get rich, so that the desire is strong enough to hold your thoughts directed to the purpose as the magnetic pole holds the needle of the compass, it will hardly be worth while for you to try to carry out the instructions given in this book.

The methods herein set forth are for people whose desire for riches is strong enough to overcome mental laziness and the love of ease, and make them work.

The more clear and definite you make your picture, then, and the more you dwell upon it, bringing out all its delightful details, the stronger your desire will be; and the stronger your desire, the easier it will be to hold your mind fixed upon the picture of what you want.

Something more is necessary, however, than merely to see the picture clearly. If that is all you do, you are only a dreamer, and will have little or no power for accomplishment.

Behind your clear vision must be the purpose to realize it; to bring it out in tangible expression.

And behind this purpose must be an invincible and unwavering FAITH that the thing is already yours; that it is "at hand" and you have only to take possession of it.

Live in the new house, mentally, until it takes form around you physically. In the mental realm, enter at once into full enjoyment of the things you want.

"Whatsoever things ye ask for when ye pray, believe that ye receive them, and ye shall have them," said Jesus.

See the things you want as if they were actually around you all the time; see yourself as owning and using them. Make use of them in imagination just as you will use them when they are your tangible possessions. Dwell upon your mental picture until it is clear and distinct, and then take the Mental Attitude of Ownership toward everything in that picture. Take possession of it, in mind, in the full faith that it is actually yours. Hold to this mental ownership; do not waver for an instant in the faith that it is real.

And remember what was said in a preceding chapter about gratitude; be as thankful for it all the time as you expect to be when it has taken form. The man who can sincerely thank God for the things which as yet he owns only in imagination, has real faith. He will get rich; he will cause the creation of whatsoever he wants.

You do not need to pray repeatedly for the things you want; it is not necessary to tell God about it every day.

"Use not vain repetitions as the heathen do," said Jesus to His pupils, "for your Father knoweth that ye have need of these things before ye ask Him."

Your part is to intelligently formulate your desire for the things which make for a larger life, and to get these desires arranged into a coherent whole; and then to impress this Whole Desire upon the Formless Substance, which has the power and the will to bring you what you want.

You do not make this impression by repeating strings of words; you make it by holding the vision with unshakable PURPOSE to attain it, and with steadfast FAITH that you do attain it.

The answer to prayer is not according to your faith while you are talking, but according to your faith while you are working.

You cannot impress the mind of God by having a special Sabbath day set apart to tell Him what you want, and then forgetting Him during the rest of the week. You cannot impress Him by having special hours to go into your closet and pray, if you then dismiss the matter from your mind until the hour of prayer comes again.

Oral prayer is well enough, and has its effect, especially upon yourself, in clarifying your vision and strengthening your faith; but it is not your oral petitions which get you what you want. In order to get rich you do not need a "sweet hour of prayer"; you need to "pray without ceasing." And by prayer I mean holding steadily to your vision, with the purpose to cause its creation into solid form, and the faith that you are doing so.

"Believe that ye *receive* them."

The whole matter turns on receiving, once you have clearly formed your vision. When you *have* formed it, it is well to make an oral statement, addressing the Supreme in reverent prayer; and from that moment you must, in mind, receive what you ask for. Live in the new house; wear the fine clothes; ride in the automobile; go on the journey, and confidently plan for greater journeys. Think and speak of all the things you have asked for in terms of actual present ownership. Imagine an environment, and a financial condition exactly as you want them, and live all the time in that imaginary environment and financial condition. Mind, however, that you do not do this as a mere dreamer and castle builder; hold to the FAITH that the imaginary is being realized, and to the PURPOSE to realize it. Remember that it is faith and purpose in the use of the imagination which make the difference between the scientist and the dreamer. And having learned this fact, it is here that you must learn the proper use of the Will.

CHAPTER IX.
HOW TO USE THE WILL.

To set about getting rich in a scientific way, you do not try to apply your will power to anything outside of yourself.

You have no right to do so, anyway.

It is wrong to apply your will to other men and women, in order to get them to do what you wish done.

It is as flagrantly wrong to coerce people by mental power as it is to coerce them by physical power. If compelling people by physical force to do things for you reduces them to slavery, compelling them by mental means accomplishes exactly the same thing; the only difference is in methods. If taking things from people by physical force is robbery, then taking things by mental force is robbery also; there is no difference in principle.

You have no right to use your will power upon another person, even "for his own good"; for you do not know what is for his good.

The science of getting rich does not require you to apply power or force to any other person, in any way whatsoever. There is not the slightest necessity for doing so; indeed, any attempt to use your will upon others will only tend to defeat your purpose.

You do not need to apply your will to things, in order to compel them to come to you.

That would simply be trying to coerce God, and would be foolish and useless, as well as irreverent.

You do not have to compel God to give you good things, any more than you have to use your will power to make the sun rise.

You do not have to use your will power to conquer an unfriendly deity, or to make stubborn and rebellious forces do your bidding.

Substance is friendly to you, and is more anxious to give you what you want than you are to get it.

To get rich, you need only to use your will power upon yourself.

When you know what to think and do, then you must use your will to compel yourself to think and do the right things. That is the legitimate use of the will in getting what you want to use it in holding yourself to the right course. Use your will to keep yourself thinking and acting in the Certain Way.

Do not try to project your will, or your thoughts, or your mind out into space, to "act" on things or people.

Keep your mind at home; it can accomplish more there than elsewhere.

Use your mind to form a mental image of what you want, and to hold that vision with faith and purpose; and use your will to keep your mind working in the Right Way.

The more steady and continuous your faith and purpose, the more rapidly you will get rich, because you will make only POSITIVE impressions upon Substance; and you will not neutralize or offset them by negative impressions.

The picture of your desires, held with faith and purpose, is taken up by the Formless, and permeates it to great distances, throughout the universe, for all I know.

As this impression spreads, all things are set moving toward its realization; every living thing, every inanimate thing, and the things yet uncreated, are stirred toward bringing into being that which you want. All force begins to be exerted in that direction; all things begin to move toward you. The minds of people, everywhere, are influenced toward doing the things necessary to the fulfilling of your desires; and they work for you, unconsciously.

But you can check all this by starting a negative impression in the Formless Substance. Doubt or unbelief is as certain to start a movement away from you as faith and purpose are to start one toward you. It is by not understanding this that most people who try to make use of "mental science" in getting rich make their failure. Every hour and moment you spend in giving heed to doubts and fears, every hour you spend in worry, every hour in which your soul is possessed by unbelief, sets a current away from you in the whole domain of intelligent Substance. All the promises are unto them that believe, and unto them only. Notice how insistent Jesus was upon this point of belief; and now you know the reason why.

Since belief is all important, it behooves you to guard your thoughts; and as your beliefs will be shaped to a very great extent by the things you observe and think about, it is important that you should command your attention.

And here the will comes into use; for it is by your will that you determine upon what things your attention shall be fixed.

If you want to become rich, you must not make a study of poverty.

Things are not brought into being by thinking about their opposites. Health is never to be attained by studying disease and thinking about disease; righteousness is not to be promoted by studying sin and thinking about sin; and no one ever got rich by studying poverty and thinking about poverty.

Medicine as a science of disease has increased disease; religion as a science of sin has promoted sin, and economics as a study of poverty will fill the world with wretchedness and want.

Do not talk about poverty; do not investigate it, or concern yourself with it. Never mind what its causes are; you have nothing to do with them.

What concerns you is the cure.

Do not spend your time in charitable work, or charity movements; all charity only tends to perpetuate the wretchedness it aims to eradicate.

I do not say that you should be hard-hearted or unkind, and refuse to hear the cry of need; but you must not try to eradicate poverty in any of the conventional ways. Put poverty behind you, and put all that pertains to it behind you, and "make good."

Get rich; that is the best way you can help the poor.

And you cannot hold the mental image which is to make you rich if you fill your mind with pictures of poverty. Do not read books or papers which give circumstantial accounts of the wretchedness of the tenement dwellers, of the horrors of child labor, and so on. Do not read anything which fills your mind with gloomy images of want and suffering.

You cannot help the poor in the least by knowing about these things; and the wide-spread knowledge of them does not tend at all to do away with poverty.

What tends to do away with poverty is not the getting of pictures of poverty into your mind, but getting pictures of wealth into the minds of the poor.

You are not deserting the poor in their misery when you refuse to allow your mind to be filled with pictures of that misery.

Poverty can be done away with, not by increasing the number of well-to-do people who think about poverty, but by increasing the number of poor people who propose with faith to get rich.

The poor do not need charity; they need inspiration. Charity only sends them a loaf of bread to keep them alive in their wretchedness, or gives them an entertainment to make them forget for an hour or two; but inspiration will cause them to rise out of their misery. If you want to help the poor, demonstrate to them that they can become rich; prove it by getting rich yourself.

The only way in which poverty will ever be banished from this world is by getting a large and constantly increasing number of people to practice the teachings of this book.

People must be taught to become rich by creation, not by competition.

Every man who becomes rich by competition throws down behind him the ladder by which he rises, and keeps others down; but every man who gets rich by creation opens a way for thousands to follow him, and inspires them to do so.

You are not showing hardness of heart or an unfeeling disposition when you refuse to pity poverty, see poverty, read about poverty, or think or talk about it, or to listen to those who do talk about it. Use your will power to keep your mind OFF the subject of poverty, and to keep it fixed with faith and purpose ON the vision of what you want.

CHAPTER X.
FURTHER USE OF THE WILL.

You cannot retain a true and clear vision of wealth if you are constantly turning your attention to opposing pictures, whether they be external or imaginary.

Do not tell of your past troubles of a financial nature, if you have had them; do not think of them at all. Do not tell of the poverty of your parents, or the hardships of your early life; to do any of these things is to mentally class yourself with the poor for the time being, and it will certainly check the movement of things in your direction.

"Let the dead bury their dead," as Jesus said.

Put poverty and all things that pertain to poverty completely behind you.

You have accepted a certain theory of the universe as being correct, and are resting all your hopes of happiness on its being correct; and what can you gain by giving heed to conflicting theories?

Do not read religious books which tell you that the world is soon coming to an end; and do not read the writings of muck-rakers and pessimistic philosophers who tell you that it is going to the devil.

The world is not going to the devil; it is going to God.

It is a wonderful Becoming.

True, there may be a good many things in existing conditions which are disagreeable; but what is the use of studying them when they are certainly passing away, and when the study of them only tends to check their passing and keep them with us? Why give time and attention to things which are being removed by evolutionary growth, when you can hasten their removal only by promoting the evolutionary growth as far as your part of it goes?

No matter how horrible in seeming may be the conditions in certain countries, sections, or places, you waste your time and destroy your own chances by considering them.

You should interest yourself in the world's becoming rich.

Think of the riches the world is coming into, instead of the poverty it is growing out of; and bear in mind that the only way in which you can assist the world in growing rich is by growing rich yourself through the creative method not the competitive one.

Give your attention wholly to riches; ignore poverty.

Whenever you think or speak of those who are poor, think and speak of them as those who are becoming rich; as those who are to be congratulated rather than pitied. Then they and others will catch the inspiration, and begin to search for the way out.

Because I say that you are to give your whole time and mind and thought to riches, it does not follow that you are to be sordid or mean.

To become really rich is the noblest aim you can have in life, for it includes everything else.

On the competitive plane, the struggle to get rich is a Godless scramble for power over other men; but when we come into the creative mind, all this is changed.

All that is possible in the way of greatness and soul unfoldment, of service and lofty endeavor, comes by way of getting rich; all is made possible by the use of things.

If you lack for physical health, you will find that the attainment of it is conditional on your getting rich.

Only those who are emancipated from financial worry, and who have the means to live a care-free existence and follow hygienic practices, can have and retain health.

Moral and spiritual greatness is possible only to those who are above the competitive battle for existence; and only those who are becoming rich on the plane of creative thought are free from the degrading influences of competition. If your heart is set on domestic happiness, remember that love flourishes best where there is refinement, a high level of thought, and freedom from corrupting influences; and these are to be found only where riches are attained by the exercise of creative thought, without strife or rivalry.

You can aim at nothing so great or noble, I repeat, as to become rich; and you must fix your attention upon your mental picture of riches, to the exclusion of all that may tend to dim or obscure the vision.

You must learn to see the underlying TRUTH in all things; you must see beneath all seemingly wrong conditions the Great One Life ever moving forward toward fuller expression and more complete happiness.

It is the truth that there is no such thing as poverty; that there is only wealth.

Some people remain in poverty because they are ignorant of the fact that there is wealth for them; and these can best be taught by showing them the way to affluence in your own person and practice.

Others are poor because, while they feel that there is a way out, they are too intellectually indolent to put forth the mental effort necessary to find that way and travel it; and for these the very best thing you can do is to arouse their desire by showing them the happiness that comes from being rightly rich.

Others still are poor because, while they have some notion of science, they have become so swamped and lost in the maze of metaphysical and occult theories that they do not know which road to take. They try a mixture of many systems and fail in all. For these, again, the very best thing to do is to show the right way in your own person and practice; an ounce of doing things is worth a pound of theorizing.

The very best thing you can do for the whole world is to make the most of yourself.

You can serve God and man in no more effective way than by getting rich; that is, if you get rich by the creative method, and not by the competitive one.

Another thing. We assert that this book gives in detail the principles of the science of getting rich; and if that is true, you do not need to read any other book upon the subject. This may sound narrow and egotistical, but consider: there is no more scientific method of computation in mathematics than by addition, subtraction, multiplication, and division; no other method is possible. There can be but one shortest distance between two points. There is only one way to think scientifically, and that is to think in the way that leads by the most direct and simple route to the goal. No man has yet formulated a briefer or less complex "system" than the one set forth herein; it has been stripped of all non-essentials. When you commence on this, lay all others aside; put them out of your mind altogether.

Read this book every day; keep it with you; commit it to memory, and do not think about other "systems" and theories.

If you do, you will begin to have doubts, and to be uncertain and wavering in your thought; and then you will begin to make failures.

After you have made good and become rich, you may study other systems as much as you please; but until you are quite sure that you have gained what you want, do not read anything on this line but this book, unless it be the authors mentioned in the Preface.

And read only the most optimistic comments on the world's news; those in harmony with your picture. Also, postpone your investigations into the occult. Do not dabble in

Theosophy, Spiritualism, or kindred studies. It is very likely that the dead still live, and are near; but if they are, let them alone; mind your own business.

Wherever the spirits of the dead may be, they have their own work to do, and their own problems to solve; and we have no right to interfere with them. We cannot help them, and it is very doubtful whether they can help us, or whether we have any right to trespass upon their time if they can. Let the dead and the hereafter alone, and solve your own problem; get rich. If you begin to mix with the occult, you will start mental cross-currents which will surely bring your hopes to shipwreck.

Now, this and the preceding chapters have brought us to the following statement of basic facts:

There is a thinking stuff from which all things are made, and which, in its original state, permeates, penetrates, and fills the interspaces of the universe.

A thought, in this substance, produces the thing that is imaged by the thought.

Man can form things in his thought, and, by impressing his thought upon formless substance, can cause the thing he thinks about to be created.

In order to do this, man must pass from the competitive to the creative mind; he must form a clear mental picture of the things he wants, and hold this picture in his thoughts with the fixed PURPOSE to get what he wants, and the unwavering FAITH that he does get what he wants, closing his mind against all that may tend to shake his purpose, dim his vision, or quench his faith.

And in addition to all this, we shall now see that he must live and act in a Certain Way.

CHAPTER XI.

ACTING IN THE CERTAIN WAY.

Thought is the creative power, or the impelling force which causes the creative power to act; thinking in a Certain Way will bring riches to you, but you must not rely upon thought alone, paying no attention to personal action. That is the rock upon which many otherwise scientific metaphysical thinkers meet shipwreck--the failure to connect thought with personal action.

We have not yet reached the stage of development, even supposing such a stage to be possible, in which man can create directly from Formless Substance without nature's processes or the work of human hands; man must not only think, but his personal action must supplement his thought.

By thought you can cause the gold in the hearts of the mountains to be impelled toward you; but it will not mine itself, refine itself, coin itself into double eagles, and come rolling along the roads seeking its way into your pocket.

Under the impelling power of the Supreme Spirit, men's affairs will be so ordered that some one will be led to mine the gold for you; other men's business transactions will be so directed that the gold will be brought toward you, and you must so arrange your own business affairs that you may be able to receive it when it comes to you. Your thought makes all things, animate and inanimate, work to bring you what you want; but your personal activity must be such that you can rightly receive what you want when it reaches you. You are not to take it as charity, nor to steal it; you must give every man more in use value than he gives you in cash value.

The scientific use of thought consists in forming a clear and distinct mental image of what you want; in holding fast to the purpose to get what you want; and in realizing with grateful faith that you *do* get what you want.

Do not try to "project" your thought in any mysterious or occult way, with the idea of having it go out and do things for you; that is wasted effort, and will weaken your power to think with sanity.

The action of thought in getting rich is fully explained in the preceding chapters; your faith and purpose positively impress your vision upon Formless Substance, which has THE SAME DESIRE FOR MORE LIFE THAT YOU HAVE; and this vision, received from you, sets all the creative forces at work IN AND THROUGH THEIR REGULAR CHANNELS OF ACTION, but directed toward you.

It is not your part to guide or supervise the creative process; all you have to do with that is to retain your vision, stick to your purpose, and maintain your faith and gratitude.

But you must act in a Certain Way, so that you can appropriate what is yours when it comes to you; so that you can meet the things you have in your picture, and put them in their proper places as they arrive.

You can readily see the truth of this. When things reach you, they will be in the hands of other men, who will ask an equivalent for them.

And you can only get what is yours by giving the other man what is his.

Your pocketbook is not going to be transformed into a Fortunatus's purse, which shall be always full of money without effort on your part.

This is the crucial point in the science of getting rich; right here, where thought and personal action must be combined. There are very many people who, consciously or unconsciously, set the creative forces in action by the strength and persistence of their desires, but who remain poor because they do not provide for the reception of the thing they want when it comes.

By thought, the thing you want is brought to you; by action you receive it.

Whatever your action is to be, it is evident that you must act NOW. You cannot act in the past, and it is essential to the clearness of your mental vision that you dismiss the past from your mind. You cannot act in the future, for the future is not here yet. And you cannot tell how you will want to act in any future contingency until that contingency has arrived.

Because you are not in the right business, or the right environment now, do not think that you must postpone action until you get into the right business or environment. And do not spend time in the present taking thought as to the best course in possible future emergencies; have faith in your ability to meet any emergency when it arrives.

If you act in the present with your mind on the future, your present action will be with a divided mind, and will not be effective.

Put your whole mind into present action.

Do not give your creative impulse to Original Substance, and then sit down and wait for results; if you do, you will never get them. Act now. There is never any time but now, and there never will be any time but now. If you are ever to begin to make ready for the reception of what you want, you must begin now.

And your action, whatever it is, must most likely be in your present business or employment, and must be upon the persons and things in your present environment.

You cannot act where you are not; you cannot act where you have been, and you cannot act where you are going to be; you can act only where you are.

Do not bother as to whether yesterday's work was well done or ill done; do to-day's work well.

Do not try to do to-morrow's work now; there will be plenty of time to do that when you get to it.

Do not try, by occult or mystical means, to act on people or things that are out of your reach.

Do not wait for a change of environment before you act; get a change of environment by action.

You can so act upon the environment in which you are now, as to cause yourself to be transferred to a better environment.

Hold with faith and purpose the vision of yourself in the better environment, but act upon your present environment with all your heart, and with all your strength, and with all your mind.

Do not spend any time in day dreaming or castle building; hold to the one vision of what you want, and act NOW.

Do not cast about seeking some new thing to do, or some strange, unusual, or remarkable action to perform as a first step toward getting rich. It is probable that your actions, at least for some time to come, will be those you have been performing for some time past; but you are to begin now to perform these actions in the Certain Way, which will surely make you rich.

If you are engaged in some business, and feel that it is not the right one for you, do not wait until you get into the right business before you begin to act.

Do not feel discouraged, or sit down and lament because you are misplaced. No man was ever so misplaced but that he could find the right place, and no man ever became so involved in the wrong business but that he could get into the right business.

Hold the vision of yourself in the right business, with the purpose to get into it, and the faith that you will get into it, and are getting into it; but ACT in your present business. Use your present business as the means of getting a better one, and use your present environment as the means of getting into a better one. Your vision of the right business, if held with faith and purpose, will cause the Supreme to move the right business toward you; and your action, if performed in the Certain Way, will cause you to move toward the business.

If you are an employee, or wage earner, and feel that you must change places in order to get what you want, do not "project" your thought into space and rely upon it to get you another job. It will probably fail to do so.

Hold the vision of yourself in the job you want, while you ACT with faith and purpose on the job you have, and you will certainly get the job you want.

Your vision and faith will set the creative force in motion to bring it toward you, and your action will cause the forces in your own environment to move you toward the place you want. In closing this chapter, we will add another statement to our syllabus:

There is a thinking stuff from which all things are made, and which, in its original state, permeates, penetrates, and fills the interspaces of the universe.

A thought, in this substance, produces the thing that is imaged by the thought.

Man can form things in his thought, and, by impressing his thoughts upon formless substance, can cause the thing he thinks about to be created.

In order to do this, man must pass from the competitive to the creative mind; he must form a clear mental picture of the things he wants, and hold this picture in his thoughts with the fixed PURPOSE to get what he wants, and the unwavering FAITH that he does get what he wants, closing his mind to all that may tend to shake his purpose, dim his vision, or quench his faith.

That he may receive what he wants when it comes, man must act NOW upon the people and things in his present environment.

CHAPTER XII.
EFFICIENT ACTION.

You must use your thought as directed in previous chapters, and begin to do what you can do where you are; and you must do ALL that you can do where you are.

You can advance only by being larger than your present place; and no man is larger than his present place who leaves undone any of the work pertaining to that place.

The world is advanced only by those who more than fill their present places.

If no man quite filled his present place, you can see that there must be a going backward in everything. Those who do not quite fill their present places are a dead weight upon society, government, commerce, and industry; they must be carried along by others at a great expense. The progress of the world is retarded only by those who do not fill the places they are holding; they belong to a former age and a lower stage or plane of life, and their tendency is toward degeneration. No society could advance if every man was smaller than his place; social evolution is guided by the law of physical and mental evolution. In the animal world, evolution is caused by excess of life.

When an organism has more life than can be expressed in the functions of its own plane, it develops the organs of a higher plane, and a new species is originated.

There never would have been new species had there not been organisms which more than filled their places. The law is exactly the same for you; your getting rich depends upon your applying this principle to your own affairs.

Every day is either a successful day or a day of failure; and it is the successful days which get you what you want. If every day is a failure, you can never get rich; while if every day is a success, you cannot fail to get rich.

If there is something that may be done to-day, and you do not do it, you have failed in so far as that thing is concerned; and the consequences may be more disastrous than you imagine.

You cannot foresee the results of even the most trivial act; you do not know the workings of all the forces that have been set moving in your behalf. Much may be depending on your doing some simple act; it may be the very thing which is to open the door of opportunity to very great possibilities. You can never know all the combinations which Supreme Intelligence is making for you in the world of things and of human affairs; your neglect or failure to do some small thing may cause a long delay in getting what you want.

Do, every day, ALL that can be done that day.

There is, however, a limitation or qualification of the above that you must take into account.

You are not to overwork, nor to rush blindly into your business in the effort to do the greatest possible number of things in the shortest possible time.

You are not to try to do to-morrow's work to-day, nor to do a week's work in a day.

It is really not the number of things you do, but the EFFICIENCY of each separate action that counts.

Every act is, in itself, either a success or a failure.

Every act is, in itself, either effective or inefficient.

Every inefficient act is a failure, and if you spend your life in doing inefficient acts, your whole life will be a failure.

The more things you do, the worse for you, if all your acts are inefficient ones.

On the other hand, every efficient act is a success in itself, and if every act of your life is an efficient one, your whole life MUST be a success.

The cause of failure is doing too many things in an inefficient manner, and not doing enough things in an efficient manner.

You will see that it is a self-evident proposition that if you do not do any inefficient acts, and if you do a sufficient number of efficient acts, you will become rich. If, now, it is possible for you to make each act an efficient one, you see again that the getting of riches is reduced to an exact science, like mathematics.

The matter turns, then, on the question whether you can make each separate act a success in itself. And this you can certainly do.

You can make each act a success, because All Power is working with you; and All Power cannot fail.

Power is at your service; and to make each act efficient you have only to put power into it.

Every action is either strong or weak; and when every one is strong, you are acting in the Certain Way which will make you rich.

Every act can be made strong and efficient by holding your vision while you are doing it, and putting the whole power of your FAITH and PURPOSE into it.

It is at this point that the people fail who separate mental power from personal action. They use the power of mind in one place and at one time, and they act in another place and at another time. So their acts are not successful in themselves; too many of them are inefficient. But if All Power goes into every act, no matter how commonplace, every act will be a success in itself; and as in the nature of things every success opens the way to other successes, your progress toward what you want, and the progress of what you want toward you, will become increasingly rapid.

Remember that successful action is cumulative in its results. Since the desire for more life is inherent in all things, when a man begins to move toward larger life more things attach themselves to him, and the influence of his desire is multiplied.

Do, every day, all that you can do that day, and do each act in an efficient manner.

In saying that you must hold your vision while you are doing each act, however trivial or commonplace, I do not mean to say that it is necessary at all times to see the vision distinctly to its smallest details. It should be the work of your leisure hours to use your imagination on the details of your vision, and to contemplate them until they are firmly fixed upon your memory.

If you wish speedy results, spend practically all your spare time in this practice.

By continuous contemplation you will get the picture of what you want, even to the smallest details, so firmly fixed upon your mind, and so completely transferred to the mind of Formless Substance, that in your working hours you need only to mentally refer to the picture to stimulate your faith and purpose, and cause your best effort to be put forth. Contemplate your picture in your leisure hours until your consciousness is so full of it that you can grasp it instantly. You will become so enthused with its bright promises that the mere thought of it will call forth the strongest energies of your whole being.

Let us again repeat our syllabus, and by slightly changing the closing statements bring it to the point we have now reached.

There is a thinking stuff from which all things are made, and which, in its original state, permeates, penetrates, and fills the interspaces of the universe.

A thought, in this substance, produces the thing that is imaged by the thought.

Man can form things in his thought, and, by impressing his thought upon formless substance, can cause the thing he thinks about to be created.

In order to do this, man must pass from the competitive to the creative mind; he must form a clear mental picture of the things he wants, and do, with faith and purpose, all that can be done each day, doing each separate thing in an efficient manner.

CHAPTER XIII.

GETTING INTO THE RIGHT BUSINESS.

Success, in any particular business, depends for one thing upon your possessing in a well-developed state the faculties required in that business.

Without good musical faculty no one can succeed as a teacher of music; without well-developed mechanical faculties no one can achieve great success in any of the mechanical trades; without tact and the commercial faculties no one can succeed in mercantile pursuits. But to possess in a well-developed state the faculties required in your particular vocation does not insure getting rich. There are musicians who have remarkable talent, and who yet remain poor; there are blacksmiths, carpenters, and so on who have excellent mechanical ability, but who do not get rich; and there are merchants with good faculties for dealing with men who nevertheless fail.

The different faculties are tools; it is essential to have good tools, but it is also essential that the tools should be used in the Right Way. One man can take a sharp saw, a square, a good plane, and so on, and build a handsome article of furniture; another man can take the same tools and set to work to duplicate the article, but his production will be a botch. He does not know how to use good tools in a successful way.

The various faculties of your mind are the tools with which you must do the work which is to make you rich; it will be easier for you to succeed if you get into a business for which you are well equipped with mental tools.

Generally speaking, you will do best in that business which will use your strongest faculties; the one for which you are naturally "best fitted." But there are limitations to this statement, also. No man should regard his vocation as being irrevocably fixed by the tendencies with which he was born.

You can get rich in ANY business, for if you have not the right talent for it you can develop that talent; it merely means that you will have to make your tools as you go along, instead of confining yourself to the use of those with which you were born. It will be EASIER for you to succeed in a vocation for which you already have the talents in a well-developed state;

but you CAN succeed in any vocation, for you can develop any rudimentary talent, and there is no talent of which you have not at least the rudiment.

You will get rich most easily in point of effort, if you do that for which you are best fitted; but you will get rich most satisfactorily if you do that which you WANT to do.

Doing what you want to do is life; and there is no real satisfaction in living if we are compelled to be forever doing something which we do not like to do, and can never do what we want to do. And it is certain that you can do what you want to do; the desire to do it is proof that you have within you the power which can do it.

Desire is a manifestation of power.

The desire to play music is the power which can play music seeking expression and development; the desire to invent mechanical devices is the mechanical talent seeking expression and development.

Where there is no power, either developed or undeveloped, to do a thing, there is never any desire to do that thing; and where there is strong desire to do a thing, it is certain proof that the power to do it is strong, and only requires to be developed and applied in the

Right Way.

All things else being equal, it is best to select the business for which you have the best developed talent; but if you have a strong desire to engage in any particular line of work, you should select that work as the ultimate end at which you aim.

You can do what you want to do, and it is your right and privilege to follow the business or avocation which will be most congenial and pleasant.

You are not obliged to do what you do not like to do, and should not do it except as a means to bring you to the doing of the thing you want to do.

If there are past mistakes whose consequences have placed you in an undesirable business or environment, you may be obliged for some time to do what you do not like to do; but you can make the doing of it pleasant by knowing that it is making it possible for you to come to the doing of what you want to do.

If you feel that you are not in the right vocation, do not act too hastily in trying to get into another one. The best way, generally, to change business or environment is by growth.

Do not be afraid to make a sudden and radical change if the opportunity is presented, and you feel after careful consideration that it is the right opportunity; but never take sudden or radical action when you are in doubt as to the wisdom of doing so.

There is never any hurry on the creative plane; and there is no lack of opportunity.

When you get out of the competitive mind you will understand that you never need to act hastily. No one else is going to beat you to the thing you want to do; there is enough for all. If one place is taken, another and a better one will be opened for you a little farther on; there is plenty of time. When you are in doubt, wait. Fall back on the contemplation of your vision, and increase your faith and purpose; and by all means, in times of doubt and indecision, cultivate gratitude.

A day or two spent in contemplating the vision of what you want, and in earnest thanksgiving that you are getting it, will bring your mind into such close relationship with the Supreme that you will make no mistake when you do act.

There is a mind which knows all there is to know; and you can come into close unity with this mind by faith and the purpose to advance in life, if you have deep gratitude.

Mistakes come from acting hastily, or from acting in fear or doubt, or in forgetfulness of the Right Motive, which is more life to all, and less to none.

As you go on in the Certain Way, opportunities will come to you in increasing number; and you will need to be very steady in your faith and purpose, and to keep in close touch with the All Mind by reverent gratitude.

Do all that you can do in a perfect manner every day, but do it without haste, worry, or fear. Go as fast as you can, but never hurry.

Remember that in the moment you begin to hurry you cease to be a creator and become a competitor; you drop back upon the old plane again.

Whenever you find yourself hurrying, call a halt; fix your attention on the mental image of the thing you want, and begin to give thanks that you are getting it. The exercise of GRATITUDE will never fail to strengthen your faith and renew your purpose.

CHAPTER XIV.

THE IMPRESSION OF INCREASE.

Whether you change your vocation or not, your actions for the present must be those pertaining to the business in which you are now engaged.

You can get into the business you want by making constructive use of the business you are already established in; by doing your daily work in a Certain Way.

And in so far as your business consists in dealing with other men, whether personally or by letter, the key-thought of all your efforts must be to convey to their minds the impression of increase.

Increase is what all men and all women are seeking; it is the urge of the Formless Intelligence within them, seeking fuller expression.

The desire for increase is inherent in all nature; it is the fundamental impulse of the universe. All human activities are based on the desire for increase; people are seeking more food, more clothes, better shelter, more luxury, more beauty, more knowledge, more pleasure--increase in something, more life.

Every living thing is under this necessity for continuous advancement; where increase of life ceases, dissolution and death set in at once.

Man instinctively knows this, and hence he is forever seeking more. This law of perpetual increase is set forth by Jesus in the parable of the talents; only those who gain more retain any; from him who hath not shall be taken away even that which he hath.

The normal desire for increased wealth is not an evil or a reprehensible thing; it is simply the desire for more abundant life; it is aspiration.

And because it is the deepest instinct of their natures, all men and women are attracted to him who can give them more of the means of life.

In following the Certain Way as described in the foregoing pages, you are getting continuous increase for yourself, and you are giving it to all with whom you deal.

You are a creative center, from which increase is given off to all.

Be sure of this, and convey assurance of the fact to every man, woman, and child with whom you come in contact. No matter how small the transaction, even if it be only the selling of a stick of candy to a little child, put into it the thought of increase, and make sure that the customer is impressed with the thought.

Convey the impression of advancement with everything you do, so that all people shall receive the impression that you are an Advancing Man, and that you advance all who deal with you. Even to the people whom you meet in a social way, without any thought of business, and to whom you do not try to sell anything, give the thought of increase.

You can convey this impression by holding the unshakable faith that you, yourself, are in the Way of Increase; and by letting this faith inspire, fill, and permeate every action.

Do everything that you do in the firm conviction that you are an advancing personality, and that you are giving advancement to everybody.

Feel that you are getting rich, and that in so doing you are making others rich, and conferring benefits on all.

Do not boast or brag of your success, or talk about it unnecessarily; true faith is never boastful.

Wherever you find a boastful person, you find one who is secretly doubtful and afraid. Simply feel the faith, and let it work out in every transaction; let every act and tone and look express the quiet assurance that you are getting rich; that you are already rich. Words will not be necessary to communicate this feeling to others; they will feel the sense of increase when in your presence, and will be attracted to you again.

You must so impress others that they will feel that in associating with you they will get increase for themselves. See that you give them a use value greater than the cash value you are taking from them.

Take an honest pride in doing this, and let everybody know it; and you will have no lack of customers. People will go where they are given increase; and the Supreme, which desires increase in all, and which knows all, will move toward you men and women who have never heard of you. Your business will increase rapidly, and you will be surprised at the unexpected benefits which will come to you. You will be able from day to day to make larger combinations, secure greater advantages, and to go on into a more congenial vocation if you desire to do so.

But in doing all this, you must never lose sight of your vision of what you want, or your faith and purpose to get what you want.

Let me here give you another word of caution in regard to motives.

Beware of the insidious temptation to seek for power over other men.

Nothing is so pleasant to the unformed or partially developed mind as the exercise of power or dominion over others. The desire to rule for selfish gratification has been the curse of the world. For countless ages kings and lords have drenched the earth with blood in their battles to extend their dominions; this not to seek more life for all, but to get more power for themselves.

To-day, the main motive in the business and industrial world is the same; men marshal their armies of dollars, and lay waste the lives and hearts of millions in the same mad scramble for power over others. Commercial kings, like political kings, are inspired by the lust for power.

Jesus saw in this desire for mastery the moving impulse of that evil world He sought to overthrow. Read the twenty-third chapter of Matthew, and see how He pictures the lust of the Pharisees to be called "Master," to sit in the high places, to domineer over others, and to lay burdens on the backs of the less fortunate; and note how He compares this lust for dominion with the brotherly seeking for the Common Good to which He calls His disciples.

Look out for the temptation to seek for authority, to become a "master," to be considered as one who is above the common herd, to impress others by lavish display, and so on.

The mind that seeks for mastery over others is the competitive mind; and the competitive mind is not the creative one. In order to master your environment and your destiny, it is not at all necessary that you should rule over your fellow men; and indeed, when you fall into the world's struggle for the high places, you begin to be conquered by fate and environment, and your getting rich becomes a matter of chance and speculation.

Beware of the competitive mind! No better statement of the principle of creative action can be formulated than the favorite declaration of the late "Golden Rule" Jones of Toledo: "What I want for myself, I want for everybody."

CHAPTER XV.

THE ADVANCING MAN.

What I have said in the last chapter applies as well to the professional man and the wage-earner as to the man who is engaged in mercantile business.

No matter whether you are a physician, a teacher, or a clergyman, if you can give increase of life to others and make them sensible of the fact, they will be attracted to you, and you will get rich. The physician who holds the vision of himself as a great and successful healer, and who works toward the complete realization of that vision with faith and purpose, as described in former chapters, will come into such close touch with the Source of Life that he will be phenomenally successful; patients will come to him in throngs.

No one has a greater opportunity to carry into effect the teachings of this book than the practitioner of medicine; it does not matter to which of the various schools he may belong, for the principle of healing is common to all of them, and may be reached by all alike. The Advancing Man in medicine, who holds to a clear mental image of himself as successful, and who obeys the laws of faith, purpose, and gratitude, will cure every curable case he undertakes, no matter what remedies he may use.

In the field of religion, the world cries out for the clergyman who can teach his hearers the true science of abundant life. He who masters the details of the science of getting rich, together with the allied sciences of being well, of being great, and of winning love, and who teaches these details from the pulpit, will never lack for a congregation. This is the gospel that the world needs; it will give increase of life, and men will hear it gladly, and will give liberal support to the man who brings it to them.

What is now needed is a demonstration of the science of life from the pulpit. We want preachers who can not only tell us how, but who in their own persons will show us how. We need the preacher who will himself be rich, healthy, great, and beloved, to teach us how to attain to these things; and when he comes he will find a numerous and loyal following.

The same is true of the teacher who can inspire the children with the faith and purpose of the advancing life. He will never be "out of a job." And any teacher who has this faith and purpose can give it to his pupils; he cannot help giving it to them if it is part of his own life and practice.

What is true of the teacher, preacher, and physician is true of the lawyer, dentist, real estate man, insurance agent--of everybody.

The combined mental and personal action I have described is infallible; it cannot fail. Every man and woman who follows these instructions steadily, perseveringly, and to the letter, will get rich. The law of the Increase of Life is as mathematically certain in its operation as the law of gravitation; getting rich is an exact science.

The wage-earner will find this as true of his case as of any of the others mentioned. Do not feel that you have no chance to get rich because you are working where there is no visible opportunity for advancement, where wages are small and the cost of living high. Form your clear mental vision of what you want, and begin to act with faith and purpose.

Do all the work you can do, every day, and do each piece of work in a perfectly successful manner; put the power of success, and the purpose to get rich, into everything that you do.

But do not do this merely with the idea of currying favor with your employer, in the hope that he, or those above you, will see your good work and advance you; it is not likely that they will do so.

The man who is merely a "good" workman, filling his place to the very best of his ability, and satisfied with that, is valuable to his employer; and it is not to the employer's interest to promote him; he is worth more where he is.

To secure advancement, something more is necessary than to be too large for your place.

The man who is certain to advance is the one who is too big for his place, and who has a clear concept of what he wants to be; who knows that he can become what he wants to be, and who is determined to BE what he wants to be.

Do not try to more than fill your present place with a view to pleasing your employer; do it with the idea of advancing yourself. Hold the faith and purpose of increase during work hours, after work hours, and before work hours. Hold it in such a way that every person who comes in contact with you, whether foreman, fellow workman, or social acquaintance, will feel the power of purpose radiating from you; so that every one will get the sense of advancement and increase from you. Men will be attracted to you, and if there is no possibility for advancement in your present job, you will very soon see an opportunity to take another job.

There is a Power which never fails to present opportunity to the Advancing Man who is moving in obedience to law.

God cannot help helping you, if you act in a Certain Way; He must do so in order to help Himself.

There is nothing in your circumstances or in the industrial situation that can keep you down. If you cannot get rich working for the steel trust, you can get rich on a ten-acre farm; and if you begin to move in the Certain Way, you will certainly escape from the "clutches" of the steel trust and get on to the farm or wherever else you wish to be.

If a few thousands of its employees would enter upon the Certain Way, the steel trust would soon be in a bad plight; it would have to give its workingmen more opportunity, or go out of business. Nobody has to work for a trust; the trusts can keep men in so-called hopeless conditions only so long as there are men who are too ignorant to know of the science of getting rich, or too intellectually slothful to practice it.

Begin this way of thinking and acting, and your faith and purpose will make you quick to see any opportunity to better your condition.

Such opportunities will speedily come, for the Supreme, working in All, and working for you, will bring them before you.

Do not wait for an opportunity to be all that you want to be; when an opportunity to be more than you are now is presented and you feel impelled toward it, take it. It will be the first step toward a greater opportunity.

There is no such thing possible in this universe as a lack of opportunities for the man who is living the advancing life.

It is inherent in the constitution of the cosmos that all things shall be for him and work together for his good; and he must certainly get rich if he acts and thinks in the Certain Way. So let wage-earning men and women study this book with great care, and enter with confidence upon the course of action it prescribes; it will not fail.

CHAPTER XVI.
SOME CAUTIONS, AND CONCLUDING OBSERVATIONS.

Many people will scoff at the idea that there is an exact science of getting rich; holding the impression that the supply of wealth is limited, they will insist that social and governmental institutions must be changed before even any considerable number of people can acquire a competence.

But this is not true.

It is true that existing governments keep the masses in poverty, but this is because the masses do not think and act in the Certain Way.

If the masses begin to move forward as suggested in this book, neither governments nor industrial systems can check them; all systems must be modified to accommodate the forward movement.

If the people have the Advancing Mind, have the Faith that they can become rich, and move forward with the fixed purpose to become rich, nothing can possibly keep them in poverty.

Individuals may enter upon the Certain Way at any time, and under any government, and make themselves rich; and when any considerable number of individuals do so under any government, they will cause the system to be so modified as to open the way for others.

The more men who get rich on the competitive plane, the worse for others; the more who get rich on the creative plane, the better for others.

The economic salvation of the masses can only be accomplished by getting a large number of people to practice the scientific method set down in this book, and become rich. These will show others the way, and inspire them with a desire for real life, with the faith that it can be attained, and with the purpose to attain it.

For the present, however, it is enough to know that neither the government under which you live nor the capitalistic or competitive system of industry can keep you from getting rich. When you enter upon the creative plane of thought you will rise above all these things and become a citizen of another kingdom.

But remember that your thought must be held upon the creative plane; you are never for an instant to be betrayed into regarding the supply as limited, or into acting on the moral level of competition.

Whenever you do fall into old ways of thought, correct yourself instantly; for when you are in the competitive mind, you have lost the co-operation of the Mind of the Whole.

Do not spend any time in planning as to how you will meet possible emergencies in the future, except as the necessary policies may affect your actions to-day. You are concerned with doing to-day's work in a perfectly successful manner, and not with emergencies which may arise to-morrow; you can attend to them as they come.

Do not concern yourself with questions as to how you shall surmount obstacles which may loom upon your business horizon, unless you can see plainly that your course must be altered to-day in order to avoid them.

No matter how tremendous an obstruction may appear at a distance, you will find that if you go on in the Certain Way it will disappear as you approach it, or that a way over, through, or around it will appear.

No possible combination of circumstances can defeat a man or woman who is proceeding to get rich along strictly scientific lines. No man or woman who obeys the law can fail to get rich, any more than one can multiply two by two and fail to get four.

Give no anxious thought to possible disasters, obstacles, panics, or unfavorable combinations of circumstances; it is time enough to meet such things when they present themselves before you in the immediate present, and you will find that every difficulty carries with it the wherewithal for its overcoming.

Guard your speech. Never speak of yourself, your affairs, or of anything else in a discouraged or discouraging way.

Never admit the possibility of failure, or speak in a way that infers failure as a possibility.

Never speak of the times as being hard, or of business conditions as being doubtful. Times may be hard and business doubtful for those who are on the competitive plane, but they can never be so for you; you can create what you want, and you are above fear.

When others are having hard times and poor business, you will find your greatest opportunities.

Train yourself to think of and to look upon the world as a something which is Becoming, which is growing; and to regard seeming evil as being only that which is undeveloped. Always speak in terms of advancement; to do otherwise is to deny your faith, and to deny your faith is to lose it.

Never allow yourself to feel disappointed. You may expect to have a certain thing at a certain time, and not get it at that time; and this will appear to you like failure.

But if you hold to your faith you will find that the failure is only apparent.

Go on in the certain way, and if you do not receive that thing, you will receive something so much better that you will see that the seeming failure was really a great success.

A student of this science had set his mind on making a certain business combination which seemed to him at the time to be very desirable, and he worked for some weeks to bring it about. When the crucial time came, the thing failed in a perfectly inexplicable way; it was as if some unseen influence had been working secretly against him. He was not disappointed; on the contrary, he thanked God that his desire had been overruled, and went steadily on with a grateful mind. In a few weeks an opportunity so much better came his way that he would not have made the first deal on any account; and he saw that a Mind which knew more than he knew had prevented him from losing the greater good by entangling himself with the lesser.

That is the way every seeming failure will work out for you, if you keep your faith, hold to your purpose, have gratitude, and do, every day, all that can be done that day, doing each separate act in a successful manner.

When you make a failure, it is because you have not asked for enough; keep on, and a larger thing than you were seeking will certainly come to you. Remember this.

You will not fail because you lack the necessary talent to do what you wish to do. If you go on as I have directed, you will develop all the talent that is necessary to the doing of your work.

It is not within the scope of this book to deal with the science of cultivating talent; but it is as certain and simple as the process of getting rich.

However, do not hesitate or waver for fear that when you come to any certain place you will fail for lack of ability; keep right on, and when you come to that place, the ability will be furnished to you. The same source of Ability which enabled the untaught Lincoln to do the greatest work in government ever accomplished by a single man is open to you; you may draw upon all the mind there is for wisdom to use in meeting the responsibilities which are laid upon you. Go on in full faith.

Study this book. Make it your constant companion until you have mastered all the ideas contained in it. While you are getting firmly established in this faith, you will do well to give up most recreations and pleasures; and to stay away from places where ideas conflicting with these are advanced in lectures or sermons. Do not read pessimistic or conflicting literature, or get into arguments upon the matter. Do very little reading, outside of the writers mentioned in the Preface. Spend most of your leisure time in contemplating your vision, and in cultivating gratitude, and in reading this book. It contains all you need to know of the science of getting rich; and you will find all the essentials summed up in the following chapter.

CHAPTER XVII.

SUMMARY OF THE SCIENCE OF GETTING RICH.

There is a thinking stuff from which all things are made, and which, in its original state, permeates, penetrates, and fills the interspaces of the universe.

A thought in this substance produces the thing that is imaged by the thought.

Man can form things in his thought, and by impressing his thought upon formless substance can cause the thing he thinks about to be created.

In order to do this, man must pass from the competitive to the creative mind; otherwise he cannot be in harmony with the Formless Intelligence, which is always creative and never competitive in spirit.

Man may come into full harmony with the Formless Substance by entertaining a lively and sincere gratitude for the blessings it bestows upon him. Gratitude unifies the mind of man with the intelligence of Substance, so that man's thoughts are received by the Formless. Man can remain upon the creative plane only by uniting himself with the Formless Intelligence through a deep and continuous feeling of gratitude.

Man must form a clear and definite mental image of the things he wishes to have, to do, or to become; and he must hold this mental image in his thoughts, while being deeply grateful to the Supreme that all his desires are granted to him. The man who wishes to get rich must spend his leisure hours in contemplating his Vision, and in earnest thanksgiving that the reality is being given to him. Too much stress cannot be laid on the importance of frequent contemplation of the mental image, coupled with unwavering faith and devout gratitude. This is the process by which the impression is given to the Formless, and the creative forces set in motion.

The creative energy works through the established channels of natural growth, and of the industrial and social order. All that is included in his mental image will surely be brought to the man who follows the instructions given above, and whose faith does not waver. What he wants will come to him through the ways of established trade and commerce.

In order to receive his own when it shall come to him, man must be active; and this activity can only consist in more than filling his present place. He must keep in mind the Purpose to get rich through the realization of his mental image. And he must do, every day, all that can be done that day, taking care to do each act in a successful manner. He must give to every man a use value in excess of the cash value he receives, so that each transaction makes for more life; and he must so hold the Advancing Thought that the impression of Increase will be communicated to all with whom he comes in contact.

The men and women who practice the foregoing instructions will certainly get rich; and the riches they receive will be in exact proportion to the definiteness of their vision, the fixity of their purpose, the steadiness of their faith, and the depth of their gratitude.

We'd Love to Hear From You!

Thank you so much for reading this book-it means the world to me. If you found it helpful, inspiring, or just enjoyable, would you take a moment to leave a review? Your feedback not only helps others but also keeps me motivated to create more valuable content for you.

Here's how you can leave a review:

1. Scan the QR code on this page to go directly to the author's page.

2. Or, visit your Amazon Orders page, find this book, and click "Write a Product Review."

**Your kind words make a big difference.
Thank you for your support!**